Paths are Many Truth is One

Paths are Many Truth is One

A JOURNEY TO THE ESSENCE OF SPIRITUALITY AND RELIGION

S. G. McKeever

Editors: Mairi McKeever
Dhririta Ferency
Terry Eldredge
Islamic Consultant: Dr. Mohamad Yakan
Cover Design: Marina Woods
Interior Design: Jonathan Parker
Front Cover Photo: Parichoy Bradshaw
Back Cover Photo: Astika Mason

ISBN 1-885479-01-8

For additional information contact:
McKeever Publishing
P.O. Box 161167
San Diego, California 92176

MCKEEVER
M
PUBLISHING

San Diego • San Francisco • San Anselmo

Contents

What profit has a man of all his labor at which he toils under the sun? One generation passes away and another generation comes; but the earth abides forever. The sun rises and the sun goes down and hastens to the place where it rose that from thence it may rise again. The wind blows toward the south, and turns about to the north; it whirls continually, and returns again according to its circuits. All the rivers run into the sea, yet the sea is not full; to the place from whence the rivers flow, thither they return to flow again. All things are wearisome: a man is not satisfied with utterance, his eye is not satisfied with seeing, nor his ear satisfied with hearing. The thing that has been is that which shall be; and that which has been done is that which shall be done; and there is nothing new under the sun.

ECCLESIASTES 1:3–9

1

Paths and Truth

One Perfect Road

*There is only one perfect road
And that road is ahead of you
Always ahead of you.*

—SRI CHINMOY

Paths are many, Truth is one.

The purpose of this book is not to espouse any particular philosophy or view of spirituality, but rather to show the essential unity of the major spiritual teachings and philosophies.

Throughout the ages many prophets have come to offer guidance to those seeking Truth and God. Each of these spiritual teachers has molded their message to speak particularly to their moment in history and yet, all have taught the same essential message. It is that essence that this work is attempting to illustrate and bring forth.

Although the teachings of Jesus assume a significant role in this writing, it must be noted that the author does not consider Him to be the only true spiritual teacher. Jesus was a great spiritual teacher, among the greatest, but not the only teacher of that caliber. Mankind's spiritual growth has been guided by teachers of many races, nations and times. These teachers have spoken uniquely to their age, yet a common thread can be seen to run throughout their lives and teachings.

No single individual, philosophy, religion or teacher holds exclusive rights to the truths of life. To believe so would be to invalidate the feelings and experiences of billions of people throughout history.

Many roads lead to Rome. So too, there are many different paths of action and understanding that lead to Truth. In fact, ultimately, there are as many ways of experiencing Truth as there are individuals. Each of us must make our own way through the experiences and situations that life presents us.

If we look at any of humanity's major religions we find at its root a man or woman seeking the highest Truth: Jesus fasting and praying in the desert; Siddhartha Gautama, the Buddha, meditating under the Bodhi Tree and many others.

Unfortunately with time, the initial Truth which they expressed often becomes steeped in dogma and superstition as a result of the greed and desires of others. It is the task of each seeker to separate the true teachings from the interpretations, to find the essential truths buried beneath the ideas of others.

The ultimate Truth to which teachers point spiritual seekers has been referred to by various names by various teachers: God, Truth, Nirvana, Yahweh, Allah, the Father, the Mother, Heaven and so forth. Let us not be confused by names. A river may flow through three or four different countries. People in these various countries will call the flowing water by a different name or word and yet it is still the same river. Let us travel beyond words into the realm of experience; let us explore the common thread that unites these compatible teachings.

Words, ideas and beliefs provide us with a workable blueprint of reality, although they cannot fully represent existence. What we need to satisfy our inner hunger for higher knowledge is not words but rather direct experience. To read about mountain climbing is a far cry from actually climbing a mountain.

Beliefs based on the ideas of others soon break down under the pressures and difficult experiences we face in life. Death is a good example. To believe in heaven or reincarnation gives us a feeling of security, yet upon the death of someone we love our theories crumble into a sea of sorrow. It is only knowledge based on our direct experience that can help us with difficult moments in our lives. If one actually knew, from direct experience, what happens at the moment of death, that knowledge would replace the despair of unknowing. From the teachings of spiritual masters we should seek the inspiration and guidance to experience the ultimate Truth for ourselves. I have chosen a variety of sources upon which to build this book.

Each chapter begins with a poem by contemporary spiritual teacher Sri Chinmoy. The message of the poem is then explored through the Upanishads, the Bhagavad-Gita, the Dhammapada, the Old Testament, the Gospels of Matthew, Mark, Luke and John, the teachings of the Chinese philosopher Lao Tzu, and Islamic teachings from the Koran. I will now give you a brief introduction to each of these.

It is my suggestion that you begin each chapter by reading the opening poem two or three times and then reflect and meditate on its meaning for a few moments. Allow the feeling and your interpretation of the poem to resonate within yourself; then continue reading.

The Upanishads

The *Upanishads* are the oldest of the works to be cited. The exact date of their writing is unknown but various scholars place their origin between 2,000 and 20,000 B.C. No one knows exactly who wrote the Upanishads.

The Upanishads are part of a larger work entitled the Vedas. The Upanishads deal with the knowledge aspect of spirituality while the rest of the Vedas expound on work and ritual.

A key element concerning the Upanishads is that they are the recording of the first-hand experience of the Vedic seers, or sages, who wrote them. The truths presented are not theoretical, but believed to be based on first-hand experience. These are the oldest spiritual writings known to man and are the basis of Hinduism. The Upanishads are divided into chapters or books, the title of each will be listed as a source of reference for the reader.

The Bhagavad-Gita

The *Bhagavad-Gita*, often referred to as the bible of Hinduism, is part of a larger epic entitled the *Mahabharata* which tells the tale of a great battle between the forces of good and evil.

The Bhagavad-Gita chronicles a discussion between two men on a battlefield just before fighting is to commence. Krishna, a warrior and a great spiritual teacher, is speaking with his student-friend Arjuna just prior to the battle.

Arjuna wonders at many of life's difficulties, complexities and apparent contradictions. Krishna resolves these questions with a timeless wisdom that continues to this day to guide the lives of millions of people.

The Bhagavad-Gita was written after the Upanishads, probably in the 5th Century, B.C., and serves to clarify many apparent contradictions in the Upanishads. Krishna, knower of Truth that he is, clarifies the Vedas and applies that wisdom to the practical difficulties facing Arjuna.

The battle into which Arjuna must enter becomes merged with the battlefield of life. Krishna's message to Arjuna speaks to all men and women compelled to activity in the world yet valuing deep spiritual feelings. One of the central themes of the Bhagavad Gita is that spiritual pursuits and understanding can go hand in hand with a life of activity and service.

All quotations in this book attributed to the dialogue between Krishna and Arjuna are taken from the Bhagavad-Gita.

The Dhammapada

Siddhartha Gautama, later known as the Buddha, or "Enlightened One," lived in India 500 years before the birth of Jesus.

He began life as a prince, sheltered from the difficulties and hardships of life. Leaving the confines of the palace he ventured into the world and saw disease, old age and death; in short, he saw the sufferings of life. Renouncing the comforts he had been born into, Siddartha sought that which is not overcome by death; he sought the eternal and indestructible essence of life.

On his journey to Nirvana—the Buddhist conception of heaven or eternal bliss—he tried many of the extreme spiritual disciplines that were popular at the time. Frustrated by circuitous routes he finally sat beneath the Bodhi tree, resolved to find Truth or perish. His meditation is said to have lasted five years, culminating with his experience of Nirvana.

As a teacher he taught the "middle path," freed from both the extremes of austerity and overindulgence in the senses.

His spiritual realization was the light that has today become one of the world's major religions: Buddhism.

The Dhammapada is one of the finest sources of the Buddha's teachings which he offered for over 40 years of his life. *Dhamma* means "the teaching;" *pada* means "the way." The teachings contained in the Dhammapada are attributed directly to the Buddha and are, therefore, one of the principal works of Buddhist philosophy and religion.

Judaism

The two major writings upon which Judaism is founded are the Hebrew Bible and the *Talmud*. The Hebrew Bible is the Old Testament of the Christian Bible. The first five books of the Hebrew Bible are called the Five Books of Moses or the Torah and are considered the most important of all Jewish scripture.

The Talmud is composed of two parts: the *Mishnah*, which is believed to be the civil and religious laws given by God to Moses; and the *Gemara* which is explanations and interpretations of the these laws given by later scholars. The Mishnah was put into writing around 200 A.D. The Gemara was composed between 200 and 500 A.D.

The version of the Hebrew Bible I will quote in this writing is the 1933 translation from the Aramaic by George M. Lamsa. The reasons I have chosen this translation are given in this chapter, in the section covering the Gospels.

The Hebrew Bible, composed of 39 books, begins with the book of Genesis wherein a story of creation is told, and concludes some 1000 pages later with the prophet Malachi foretelling of the return of the great prophet Elijah. The Hebrew Bible is alive with the trials and tribulations of the Jewish people as they seek the freedom to live their sacred covenant with God.

To trace the beginnings of Judaism we need to journey back to the Mesopotamian world of 2000 B.C. This area, centered around the Tigris and Euphrates Rivers was dominated by Babylonian culture. Religious beliefs were centered around a highly complex system of nature-gods and city-gods who protected certain geographical areas but whose power was limited to those regions.

Various wandering tribes also lived in this area. Each of these clans or tribes had its own particular clan-god who accompanied the tribe on its journeys. The clan did not believe its god to be the only god, yet its god was the only one who remained loyal to and protected a particular clan.

The story of the Jewish people began in 1900 B.C. in the city of Ur, situated along the Euphrates River a few hundred miles south of Babylon. It was from here that a clan leader named Abraham, commanded by the voice of "El Shaddai" (translated: God of the Mountain), led three hundred people away from the land of pagan gods towards the promised land, where he and his descendants could worship, in freedom, the one and only God. The covenant which God made with Abraham is recorded in the first book of the Books of Moses—Genesis.

These semi-nomadic people settled themselves in Canaan, a fertile region between the

Jordan River and the Mediterranean. Here we find the beginnings of Jewish culture, a culture focused on a profound religious awareness. We are told much of Abraham and his descendents in Genesis. The First Book of Moses ends with the death of Joseph, Abraham's great, great grandson.

Exodus, the second book of the Old Testament, begins after an interlude of 400 years. By 1200 B.C. the Hebrews had become enslaved under the powerful Egyptian Pharoahs—most notably Seti I and his son Rameses II.

Moses, a Hebrew reared in the court of the Pharaoh, but living as a shepherd herding his flock in the Sinai Peninsula, was called by God to lead His people away from slavery and Egypt and return them to the Promised Land. Moses and his brother Aaron led the exodus of 5000 Hebrews. Upon Mount Sinai Moses received the Law and made a covenant forever binding Israel to God.

The Hebrew Bible goes on to tell the story of the Israelites, their return to Canaan and the subsequent ups and downs of Hebrew power and culture. Great prophets and philosopher-kings such as Joshua, Saul, Solomon, Elijah, Isaiah, Jeremiah and Ezekiel led the people through difficult and trying times. These prophets not only spoke of God but spoke to God. As a result of their direct communion with God they were able to offer their people a guiding light by which to traverse the difficulties of this world.

Judaism is the bond of unity felt between a people and their realization of a God with whom their ancestors, and themselves, have made a sacred covenant.

As we find in the Qu'ran, much of the Hebrew Bible is an attempt to move people away from pagan and polytheistic beliefs and practices. The prophets sought to create a new culture centered around the belief in an ever-present, loving and approachable God who would care for His people if certain beliefs and practices were upheld.

All seekers of Truth can benefit from the spiritual wisdom of these teachers and prophets.

Jesus

No spiritual teacher is more well known to the Western world than Jesus. It is upon His birth that we have begun our calendar, and, by inference, our age.

Jesus preached His spiritual realization and awakening for only three years, before being crucified by those whose power, fame and wealth were threatened by Jesus' doctrine of love and compassion. Jesus did not write down His own teachings and words. They were recorded by others many years later.

The Gospels

To offer, as clearly as possible, the teachings of Jesus, I have turned to the Gospels of the New Testament. There are four books which make up the Gospels. The actual authors are unknown but have been associated with two of Christ's apostles: Matthew and John, and two companions of the apostles: Mark and Luke.

Scholars generally agree that the Gospel of Mark was written first, around 70 A.D.; Matthew and Luke wrote theirs shortly after. The contents of these last two indicate that they each knew of Mark's Gospel but not of each other's. John's Gospel was written last, probably in 90 A.D.

The version of the Bible I have chosen for this writing is George M. Lamsa's 1933 translation from the Aramaic language of the Peshitta. Although the differences between this and the traditional King James version are slight, I felt that for authenticity and clarity the translation from the Aramaic should be used. My reason follows:

Jesus and his followers spoke Aramaic. Although they knew Hebrew, the language of the people at the time was Aramaic. The first Gospels were written in Aramaic and Hebrew. Documents used by the writers of the New Testament were written in Aramaic. Aramaic was the language of Christianity which spread east. The Holy Bible of the Church of the East is called the Peshitta. The Assyrian Church, or Church of the East, was the most powerful foundation for Christianity until the 14th Century. It is this version of the Bible, from the Original Aramaic, that Mr. Lamsa has translated.

By contrast let us note the development of the King James version of the Bible used today in Western culture.

While the Aramaic translation of the Bible remained intact with few revisions, it was also translated from Aramaic and Hebrew into Greek. Latin translations of the Bible from Hebrew and Greek versions began to appear in the A.D. 100's. In the A.D. 400's a Latin version was created known as the *Vulgate*, a Latin word meaning "popular." This was the only version authorized by the Roman Catholic Church.

In the 1500's, the first English translation of the Bible, authorized by Roman Catholics, was made from the Latin. In 1604, King James I of England authorized a committee of 50 scholars to prepare an authoritative version of the Bible in English. For 200 years this proved to be the version for the English-speaking world.

In the 1800's, as more became known about original Greek and Hebrew Biblical texts and ancient Near Eastern languages, many errors were uncovered in the King James' translation. Scholars and religious leaders called for new translations but few were allowed to come forward.

Most modern English translations of the Bible, although updating the manner of speech and presentation, are still derived from the original King James' version.

It is my feeling that the English translation from the Aramaic holds truer to the actual teachings of Jesus as it has suffered fewer translations and revisions at the hands of those prone to manipulate the teachings of Jesus to serve their self-interests. The scholar or interested reader can compare the passages herein with the same passages in the King James version.

The Qur'an

As the Bible is to Christians, the Qur'an is to Muslims. It is also spelt Koran.

The Prophet Muhammad lived from 570 to 632. The angel Gabriel revealed the Qur'an to Muhammed over the course of the 22 years of his preaching. The first revelation came as Muhammed was meditating alone in a cave on Mount Hora. He was 40 years old at the time.

Arabia, at the time of Muhammed, was a wild and lawless land; the various tribes of the desert were constantly at war. Pagan religions dominated the minds and lives of the people. Muhammed could not read or write. The teachings of God, revealed through the Prophet, were written down by those accepting the message of Muhammed. Only twenty years after the death of Muhammed the standard text of the Koran was completed; it consists of verses grouped into 114 chapters. For hundreds of years Muslims refused to translate the Qur'an into other languages seeking to preserve the words of God in their original form. The first translations began to appear in the early 1900's.

The central teaching of the Qur'an is that there is only one God who is responsible for all of creation. This is expressed in beautifully poetic words and imagery:

It is He who sends down water from the skies, and brings out of it everything that grows, the green foliage, the grain lying close, the date palm trees with clusters of dates, and the gardens of grapes, and of olives and pomegranates, so similar yet so unlike. Look at the fruits, how they appear on the trees, and they ripen. In all these are signs for those who believe.

—6:99

The word for God in Arabic is Allah. Allah is the creator of the universe and requires "Islam" (submission and surrender) to Himself. Muslims consider the Qur'an to be the words of God and in no sense the composition of Muhammed. They believe the earthly book to be a copy of an eternal book kept in Heaven. Allah, in His mercy, sent the Qur'an as a guide for humanity.

In addition to the central theme of one God, the Qur'an offers moral and ethical guidelines which addressed many of the social ills prevalent in Arabia at the time. The Qur'an, preached to man through Muhammed, abolished idol worship and the killing of unwanted baby girls, established laws and a system of justice and sought to shed wisdom upon the issues of prayer, fasting, war, divorce, marriage, slavery and service to the poor.

The Qur'an embraces Christianity and Judaism in that it often references the prophets and teachings of the Old and New Testaments. Jesus is, in fact, quoted many times in the Qur'an. Passages of conversation between God and Jesus seek to clarify various teachings.

Unfortunately, this oneness with Christianity is short-lived for although seeing Jesus as a great prophet the Qur'an says:

The Christ, son of Mary, was but an apostle and many apostles had come and gone before him.

—5:75

Obviously, this statement will not endear the Qur'an to those who believe Jesus to be the only Son of God.

Muslims believe Muhammed to be the last of these prophets. This belief stems from a line in the Qur'an where Muhammed is proclaimed the "seal of the prophets." (33:40) This has been interpreted to mean the last prophet, although other interpretations could be given.

A central division took place in the Muslim religion regarding the nature of Muhammed. Some, the Shites, regard Muhammed as possessing a divine nature. Others, the Sunnites, feel that he was simply a man, not endowed with any type of divine nature. A similar rift occurred in the early Christian church. Those believing Jesus to be of a divine nature won out and effectively silenced the opposing idea.

Regardless of the interpretation of various passages and metaphysical questions regarding men and prophets, the Qur'an, as do all truly spiritual philosophies, demands that all seek to fathom the depths within themselves:

Meditate on your Lord inwardly with humility and fear.

—7:205

And, as we will find throughout the history of spiritual literature, the Qur'an seeks to guide mankind to know the greatest of all truths: that God is to be found in man:

> *The Lord said to the angels: "I am verily going to create a human being from fermented clay dried tingling hard; and when I have fashioned him and breathed into him of my spirit, bow before him in homage."*
> —15:28–29

Through beautiful language and tangible sensuous imagery the Qur'an invites us to seek and know that breath of God within each one of us.

Taoism

Lao Tzu walked the soil of ancient China six centuries before the birth of Jesus. His teachings of the Tao, "the Way," have survived through the centuries and offer spiritual guidance for untold millions of people.

Lao Tzu, which means "Old Teacher," began as an archivist at the royal court of Chou. At that time China was divided into seven power-hungry courts. Lao Tzu, seeing the corruption and decline coming to the dynasty he served, withdrew to the mountains and solitude of Western China.

Confucius, who would become a great teacher of ethics and morality, met Lao Tzu when the mystic was in his 80's. Confucius, still in his 30's, wrote of the meeting:

> *Of the bird, I know that he can fly; of the fish, I know that he can swim. . . but the dragon, I know nothing of him: he rises to the sky on the clouds and the wind. Today, I have seen Lao Tzu, he is like the dragon.*

The teachings of Lao Tzu are recorded in 5000 characters said to be penned by the teacher himself. This work is today called the *Tao Te Ching*, and is traditionally divided into 2 parts and 81 short chapters. The first part deals with the *tao:* the way; the second part with *te:* virtue and power.

Lao Tzu teaches the natural order at the root of all life—the Tao—and the potential of all men to become merged in that eternal flow. One begins to enter that flow through the cultivation of humility, understanding, kindness, goodness, and other such qualities. It is not achieved through self-agradisement, power or money. He writes:

> *Leave all things to take their natural course, and do not interfere. Do nothing by self-will, but rather conform to the Infinite Will, and everything will be done for you.*

Lao Tzu found the ideal expression for his teachings in the ways of nature:

The highest form of goodness is like water. Water knows how to benefit all things without striving with them. It stays in places loathed by all men. Therefore, it comes near the Tao.

Lao Tzu describes the state of inner peace and connectedness with creation as "inaction." This does not describe a state of laziness or sloth, but rather a quieting of the ego's endless desire-stream and an awareness of life's great flow. He describes this principle:

It is the way of Heaven not to strive, and yet it knows how to overcome; not to speak, and yet it knows how to obtain a response; it calls not, and things come of themselves; it is slow to move, but excellent in its designs.

As in the tradition of all great spiritual teachers, Lao Tzu teaches the ultimate union of Heaven and earth—matter and spirit—which must be realized by each seeker. Not through a rejection of life do we find God, but through an acceptance of life and a transformation of our own awareness do we come to know the ultimate Truth. Lao Tzu writes:

These two things, the spiritual and the material, though we call them by different names, in their origin are one and the same. This sameness is a mystery—the mystery of mysteries. It is the gate of all spirituality.

Sri Chinmoy

Each prophet speaks uniquely to their age in a manner to which people can relate. Sri Chinmoy's writings and life echo the eternal spiritual truths of those who have come before him. The simplicity and power of his writings condenses great spiritual truths into a form that can be taken in by many, not just philosophers, scholars or those with backgrounds of spiritual study.

Sri Chinmoy, as a beacon for Truth, writes in a style that is accessible to all. As of this writing—1994—Sri Chinmoy has written over 1,000 books and penned over 30,000 poems. He offers a clear, concise spiritual philosophy—in his own hand—that will surely reach many future generations. He was born in India in 1931 and has made his home in New York City since 1964.

Sri Chinmoy, in his teachings and writings, espouses that God has infinite attributes and forms. One's conception of God depends entirely on one's disposition. God can be viewed as male or female, with or without form, personal or impersonal, with or without attributes, and young or old. In his writings Sri Chinmoy most often refers to God in the masculine form. This is not to present a definite form of representation; it simply reflects Sri Chinmoy's personal disposition.

The same applies to the use of the word "man." Sri Chinmoy is not limiting the feelings and ideas of his poetry to the masculine aspect of nature, but rather uses the term man to encompass both men and women—humankind.

Paths are many, Truth is One.

Spiritual teachers appear, not to create a fancy philosophy or amass a large following, but to inspire sincere seekers to find and experience the Truth of life for themselves.

It is my hope that the words and ideas presented herein offer a springboard for your own attainment of the ultimate goal of life: an awareness of the source of all creation.

There is only one perfect road
And that road is ahead of you
Always ahead of you.

2

Ego and Soul

I Know For Sure
I know for sure
That my Lord Beloved Supreme
Is not far away from me.
He is just beyond
My mind's ego screen.

—SRI CHINMOY

This poem will serve as the perfect point of departure for our venture into the realm of timeless spiritual philosophy. All philosophy begins with experience.

Words are merely representations of feelings and experiences. Life and the experience of existence are more fulfilling than the narrow confines of thought; yet we do think and seek to make sense of our existence through thought. In this first poem we encounter many of the concepts that are central to the study and experience of the mystical.

The ego is one's sense of separateness and individuality that is founded upon the mind's divisive thinking process. Ego is our sense of self that is based upon the things of this world: my job, my money, my family, my house, my community, my country, my beliefs, my experiences, my memories and my dreams. Through these relationships we arrive at a sense of individuality: my pleasure, my pain. The ego is our functioning sense of self in the realm of day-to-day living. We need an ego, a sense of self, in order to function. The question then arises as to whether this is the extent of who and what we are, or whether there is more to each person's existence. "I, me and mine" clearly define the realm of ego.

Moments of pure, deep sleep feel so good and are so emotionally and spiritually nourishing because in these moments we cease to exist. The constant thought process that revolves around "me" and "mine" is a heavy weight each of us carries through the day. It feels good to "forget" about ourselves, to think good thoughts about others, to help others, to quiet the mind and let the structure of "I, me, and mine" rest for a while.

It is also rejuvenating to "lose oneself" in an act of concentration, putting "all our attention" into something and forgetting about ourselves.

This structure of "me" and "you" is supported by thought. This structure can oscillate and change based on the thoughts that create the foundation. Ultimately, it is our thoughts that create the structure, and these thoughts are often highly dependent on our experiences as we perceive them: pain, pleasure, victory, defeat, loss, gain, and what others think or say about us adds up to create "who we are" or rather "what we think ourselves to be."

A "screen" is not very thick. Sri Chinmoy has chosen the perfect word to describe the mind's ego structure. It is thin, changing, and ultimately, quite fragile. Yet, a screen is important for it acts as a filter. Through our ego screen we filter the experiences of the world into a paradigm through which we can function.

When we allow our awareness to expand beyond this small "me," a larger, vaster awareness comes into play. This expansion of consciousness is the essence of most mystical experience.

This expanded awareness is the starting point for the journey of consciousness beyond the realm of ego. In Sri Chinmoy's poem this expanded awareness is the "I" which begins the poem. This awareness is also known as the individual soul, atman and self. From this level of consciousness there is still a sense of individuality; there is still a point of perception, but the level of awareness rises far beyond the mind's realm. We begin to enter into the realm of existence beyond the narrow confines of the mind.

From this expanded awareness—this soul awareness—we begin to connect, consciously, with God, or as Sri Chinmoy says, "The Supreme," who is, "not far away from me."

Our self, or soul-awareness, if followed to its source brings us into awareness of God, Truth, Infinity and Eternity. This journey to our Source is the essence of everyone's spiritual journey. In the Upanishads when "self" is not capitalized, it refers to the individual soul; when it is capitalized, it refers to God.

As I said earlier, all of this is merely a representation, through words, of a reality and experience far beyond thought. Let us express the same ideas through an analogy which may offer more "feeling" to our understanding. To do this we turn to the Chandogya Upanishad:

> *The rivers in the east flow eastward, the rivers in the west flow westward, and all enter into the sea. From sea to sea they pass, the clouds lifting them to the sky as vapor and sending them down as rain.*

The cycle then repeats itself. Rain drops into rivers which then flow into seas. The rain drop can be said to be the ego. The river is our soul, atman or self. The sea is the oneness of all creation. The whole process is God. This analogy could also be interpreted another way: rain is thought, river is ego, sea is soul, sky is creative force. God is the creator watching. The Qur'an speaks of God watching, knowing every movement of the creation:

I am near, and listen to the call of every supplicant the moment he calls.

—2:186

Each of us needs to find and develop our own understandings and conceptions for existence. We need a view of ourselves and life with which we feel comfortable.

Notice, though, that with each expansion—drop into river, river into sea—the experience becomes vaster and more expansive, more powerful. Mistakenly some feel that by going beyond thought or ego one will enter into an abyss of nothingness, oblivion and despair. This is not so and can be seen from the experiences conveyed by those who have journeyed beyond the ego. Jesus says this clearly as he speaks of God:

*And I know that his [God's] commandment
is life everlasting.*

—JOHN 12:50

This "life everlasting" is a conscious oneness
with God and the entire process of existence.
The rain may think it dies as it falls into the river,
yet it becomes part of the river, the rain is gone,
yet a mighty river now flows. This is the cyclical
process of life-everlasting. Life is always changing forms, yet it ceaselessly continues.

The Buddha speaks of this level of awareness
and the beauty, power and joy that awaits the
seeker who transcends the confines of the mind-
screen:

*Happy is the arising of the Awakened, happy
is the teaching of the true law, happy is the
harmony of the Order; happy is the devotion
of those who dwell in harmony.*

Everyone seeks happiness—all of us wish to
be happy. The Buddha says that the happiness
is there for those who have expanded into the
soul-awareness where the harmony of life can
be experienced. This harmony does not exist in
the realm of ego. It exists in the realm of the self.

The ego is founded upon the mind and the
thoughts spinning therein. There is little harmony in that realm. More often than not the

mind is plagued by doubt, insecurity and fear. Even the best mind is subject to the body's health. The mind, like all of physical existence, is transitory and impermanent.

Happiness and harmony exist in the realm which can be accessed only by an awareness freed from the confines of "I, me, mine." The child passes that the adult may be born. The ego too must give way to the soul if an expansion of consciousness is to continue—the expansion of the river into the sea.

Different religions and spiritual teachers conceive of these ideas through different names and forms, but ultimately all forms merge into one as Truth is perceived. Different countries may call the water drawn from a single river by different names, but in essence, they all draw the same essence: water—regardless of the word used to describe it. The Upanishads tell us:

> Man is composed of such elements as vital breath, deeds, thoughts and the senses—all of them deriving their being from the Self. They have come out of the Self, and in the Self they ultimately disappear—even as the waters of a river disappear in the sea.

The journey into the source of all creation, the journey into the essence of each and every one of us is a great undertaking. It is an uncharted journey which each of us must make for ourselves. Others may have gone before us, yet the journey is far beyond thought and ideas. Therefore, it is difficult to convey in words the journey to others.

True spiritual masters teach primarily through their lives and actions. It is difficult to speak of the world beyond the confines of speech and time.

The goal, though distant, is attainable; it is far beyond the "mind's ego-screen." Krishna, in the Bhagavad-Gita, tells his student Arjuna:

. . . supreme happiness comes to the yogi whose mind is peaceful, whose passions are at rest, who is stainless and has become one with God.

—VI: 27

Within one whose mind is at peace we find the thought waves which support the ego to be calm and tranquil. Our sense of self can then expand into the realm of pure spirit and soul. From our soul realm we are able to touch and experience the ultimate truth: God. This ultimate truth towards which we are moving is far beyond this earthly realm of transitory materialism. Jesus says this clearly:

My kingdom is not of this world.

—JOHN 19:36

Although "not of this world" it can exist within this world as the life of any great spiritual teacher will attest to. As we begin to aspire spiritually we touch a sonnet and depth within ourselves that connects us to the Infinite. Jesus tells his aspiring, seeking students:

> *If you were of this world, the world would love its own; but you are not of this world for I have chosen you out of the world.*
>
> —JOHN 15:19

To become aware of your larger sense of self, to feel the entire river and its flow towards the source, is to step beyond the awareness of the world to which most people are limited. These limits are created through our mind and thoughts. As we leave that realm we are swept, joyfully and willfully, into an existence more wonderful than we can imagine with our mind.

To step beyond our little world of "I, me, mine" is not easy; we must let go of much that makes us comfortable and secure. We need to let go of the familiar if we are to embrace the unknown. Jesus talks of this transition:

> *And every man who leaves houses or brothers or sisters or father or mother or wife or children or fields, for my name's sake, shall*

*receive a hundredfold, and shall inherit ev-
erlasting life.*

—MATTHEW 20:29

Let us not misinterpret this passage. The mere walking away from relationships and responsibilities is not what Jesus is speaking of. If it were, Jesus would not have been such an intimate companion to his mother, father and brothers, for, above all, Jesus taught through example.

The leaving of which he speaks is the letting go of ego identity. It is the inner "leaving" of which Jesus speaks: letting go of our identity as simply a son or daughter, or wife or husband or rich man or poor woman, and embracing the soul-reality. From this soul-reality we will acquire a new view of our relationship with the world. This is beautifully illustrated in Matthew:

While he was speaking to the people, his mother and his brothers came and stood outside, and wanted to speak with him.

Then a man said to him, Behold, your mother and your brothers are standing outside, and they want to speak with you.

But he answered, saying to him, who told him, Who is my mother and who are my brothers?

*And he pointed his hand to his disciples
and said, Behold my mother, and behold my
brothers.*

*For whoever does the will of my Father in
heaven is my brother and my sister and my
mother.*

—MATTHEW 12:46–50

When the smallness of our ego-bound reality
is replaced with the vastness of our soul-world,
we experience all of existence from a new vantage point. That new vision is founded on oneness and love.

*I know for sure
That my Lord Beloved Supreme
Is not far away from me.
He is just beyond
My mind's ego screen.*

For as the rain and the snow come down from heaven, and returns not thither, but waters the earth and makes it bring forth and sprout and gives seed to the sower and bread to the eater; So shall my word be that goes forth out of my mouth; it shall not return to me void, but it shall do what I please and it shall accomplish that for which I sent it. For you shall go out with joy, and be led forth with peace; the mountains and the hills shall break forth before you into singing and all the trees of the field shall clap their hands.

ISAIAH 55:10–12

3

Man and God

Although God is Infinite

Although God is Infinite
He prefers to live
Inside man's tiny heart-nest.

—SRI CHINMOY

This simple truth, that God exists within man, has been at the core of spiritual teachings for thousands of years. This truth is beautifully stated in the Chandogya Upanishad:

The light that shines above the heavens and above this world, the light that shines in the highest world, beyond which there are no oth-

ers—that is the light that shines in the hearts of men.

God, being infinite, can assume all aspects of creation and take on endless attributes. For one individual, God can take a personal form, for another, God can be impersonal, an intelligence. Depending on one's point of view or disposition, God can be power, peace, creation, destruction, calmness or pure energy. The Qur'an instructs the seeker to look at the world surrounding him or her and find the source of this marvelous creation:

Who made the earth a bed for you, the sky a canopy, and sends forth rain from the skies that fruits may grow—your food and sustenance.

—2:22

Regardless of how we perceive Him or Her, God resides within each of our hearts. The Qur'an describes this God-essence within man by describing man's creation thusly:

He breathed into him [man] of His spirit.

—32:9

The spirit of God then can be said to exist within each one of us. Although God's Breath flows throughout each cell of our existence we could say that He resides most powerfully in the core of our being—our spiritual heart. Where exactly is our spiritual heart?

The Svetasvatara Upanishad tells us:

> *He [God] envelopes the universe. Though transcendent, he is to be meditated upon as residing in the lotus of the heart, at the center of the body, ten fingers above the naval. . .*
>
> *Smaller than the smallest, greater than the greatest, the Self is hidden in the heart of all creatures.*

Our spiritual heart is our essence, that consciousness which is the motivating factor in our lives. To become aware of God within us we must keep our hearts aware of the subtle spiritual feelings and emotions within ourselves and not allow our hearts to become overwhelmed by the material world. Having a "pure heart" is the term often used by spiritual teachers to describe this type of awareness. Jesus taught those wishing to find the kingdom of heaven:

> *Sell all your possessions and give them as alms; make for yourself purses which do not wear out, and a treasure in heaven that does not run short, where the thief does not come near, and the moth does not destroy.*
>
> *For where your treasure is, there also will be your heart.*
>
> —LUKE 12:33–34

Jesus advises that we attune our hearts and lives to that which is eternal and not to that which is fleeting and transitory: that which the moth does destroy.

Again and again spiritual teachers speak of the glory and power of God; they also teach that God is within our reach, that we can become aware of the existence of God in our day-to-day lives.

This is the essence of the spiritual journey: to become conscious of the living presence of the Infinite and Eternal within our own consciousness at this very moment. This is an active role we need to play if we are to find God-awareness. The Buddha speaking to his disciples, taught:

> *You yourself must make an effort. The Buddhas are only teachers. The meditative who enter the way are freed from the bondage of Maya. [The illusion that the material realm is the only existence.]*
>
> —XX:276

The spiritual journey then is a journey into the core of our being to find the presence of God. In order to reach that awareness we must make an effort, we must discipline our awareness away from the things in life which are fleeting and focus ourselves on the spiritual, or eternal aspects of existence.

A pure heart is one of the key elements in this wonderful journey. Jesus taught:

Blessed are the pure in heart, for they shall see God.

—MATTHEW 5:8

A pure heart is synonymous with a consciousness and awareness that is not overwhelmed by the senses. The Svetasvatara Upanishad reminds us:

He is the innermost Self. He is the great Lord. It is He that reveals the purity within the heart by which he, who is pure being, may be reached. He is the ruler. He is the great light, shining forever. He is the one God, hidden in all beings, all pervading, the Self within all beings, watching over all works, dwelling in all beings.

Lao Tzu, the Chinese philosopher and founder of Taoism, describes his perception of God:

There is something, chaotic yet complete which existed before heaven and earth. Oh, how still it is and formless, standing alone without changing, reaching everywhere without suffering harm!

It must be regarded as the Mother of the Universe. Its name I know not.
   To designate it I call it Tao. Endeavoring to describe it, I call it great.

Anyone teaching that God is elsewhere than within each one of us is offering a teaching contrary to that of the great teachers who have emerged in numerous ages and cultures.

Furthermore, any individual or group claiming that God can be attained through practices which conflict with, or do not create, a feeling of purity in the heart are also deluding others. How can we know or rekindle that feeling of purity within ourselves? Perhaps Jesus put it best:

And he said, Truly I say to you, Unless you change and become like little children, you shall not enter into the kingdom of heaven.
   —MATTHEW 18:3

Let each of us awaken ourselves to the essence of all spiritual teachings:

Although God is Infinite
He prefers to live
Inside man's tiny heart-nest.

4

Jesus

If it is True

If it is true
That Jesus is coming again
Then it is also true
That you and I should go to meet Him
And welcome Him
At the halfway point.

—Sri Chinmoy

Christians throughout the world wait for the second coming of Christ, a coming that will raise the faithful to eternal life, and offer justice to those who have not heeded God's messenger.

Sri Chinmoy, in this poem, is open to the possibility of Jesus' return but then offers a challenge to all who believe and wait: that we "go to meet Him/And welcome Him/At the halfway point." Where is the halfway point, and how do we go there?

If we are here, where Jesus once stood, and he is now with the "Father in heaven" then halfway is midway between here and heaven. Even when Jesus was on earth he was able to speak to and receive messages from his Father in heaven. Jesus had access to heaven even here on Earth. Death then is not necessarily the only passage to heaven. It may be a passage, but it is not necessarily the only one: Jesus, while alive, was in communion with the Father.

Jesus said, "My kingdom is not of this world." (John 19:36) When tempted by the devil, Jesus turned down an offer to possess all the "kingdoms of the world and their glory." (Matthew 4:8) So, we know heaven is not in the physical reality of earth, but it is something we can be aware of while in the earthly realm, as Jesus was. Jesus goes on to say,

He who has seen me has seen the Father. . . the words that I speak, I do not speak of myself; but my father who abides in me does these works.

—JOHN 14:9–10

We can therefore assume that heaven and the Father exist within Jesus. In the physical absence of Jesus, which applies to our present time, Jesus says we can still access God:

But the Comforter, the Holy Spirit, whom my Father will send in my name will teach you everything, and remind you of everything which I tell you.

—JOHN 14:26

Jesus clearly tells us that in his absence we can access the Father through the Holy Spirit, for that Spirit will "remind you of everything which I tell you." Note the use of the word "everything." Among the many things which Christ taught, we can begin with two ideas that may help us access the Father:

A new commandment I give you, that you love one another; just as I have loved you, that you also love one another.

—JOHN 14:34

Jesus asks us to love. To bring an example before us that we can all cherish, Jesus, when asked who is the greatest in the kingdom of heaven says:

Truly I say to you, unless you change and become like little children, you shall not enter

into the kingdom of heaven.
Whoever therefore will humble himself like
this little child, shall be great in the kingdom
of heaven.

—MATTHEW 18:3–4

Through these two techniques, that of love and attaining the humility of a child, Jesus says we can enter the kingdom of heaven, a kingdom the Holy Spirit will guide us to—a realm within Jesus, the man, a realm within each one of us. Jesus hints at the power and access to God each of us possesses. After performing one of his miracles he says,

If you have faith and do not doubt, you will
perform a deed not only like this of the fig tree,
but should you say even to this mountain, Be
removed and fall into the sea, it shall be done.
And everything that you will ask in prayer
believing, you shall receive.

—MATTHEW 21:21

Sri Chinmoy, through his poem, challenges us to begin a journey, a journey of which we are all capable, a journey which Jesus gave us the teachings for. This is the journey through the Holy Spirit towards the kingdom of heaven. This is a journey we can begin here and now through prayer, belief, faith, love and humility.

If we do not begin to cultivate and nurture the love and humility which Jesus asks of us, why should he come again? To speak the same words to the same deaf ears? If a class of students is not listening and learning, why should the teacher continue to speak?

If we truly wish to see Jesus again, if that is what we desire with all of our hearts and souls, then it would make sense to follow the teachings he gave us to attain the kingdom of heaven. If we go halfway, possibly he will come halfway: ". . . to love one another as I have loved you."

If it is true
That Jesus is coming again
Then it is also true
That you and I should go to meet Him
And welcome Him
At the halfway point.

5

A Teacher, A Path

Only One Answer

You have a multitude of questions.
But there is only one answer:
The road is right in front of you,
And the guide is waiting for you.

—SRI CHINMOY

As we look upon ourselves and the world, our minds are besieged by an endless stream of questions concerning the meaning of life, death, the physical realm, the realm of spirit and energy, the solar system, the universe and our lives. We can spend a lifetime bouncing from one question to the next and yet never truly understand our own lives and the significance of our existence.

Sri Chinmoy has written that although we have a multitude of unanswered questions in our lives we can find the answer to any of these questions once we have answered the essential question: "Who am I?" In this poem he says to all of our questions there is but a single answer: "The road is right in front of you / And the guide is waiting for you."

To travel a road, we must begin our journey. We must take a step. To take a step we must commit to movement, to action. Many of us fear movement and changes, yet we are not alone in our search for meaning: "the guide is waiting. . ."

In any journey it is helpful to have a guide, someone who can help us in times of difficulty, to guide us along an unknown path. Often, we do not venture forth due to fear. A good guide, a teacher, quells our fear and gives us confidence during our journey.

In a spiritual quest it is helpful to have a teacher, someone to guide us towards the destination. An old Indian adage says: "When the student is ready, the teacher appears." Sri Chinmoy assures us, "the guide is waiting," yet to find the guide we must begin our journey.

How can it be that to a multitude of questions there is only one answer? Perhaps we are offered a clue to this mystery in the Isha Upanishad:

In the heart of all things, of whatever is in the universe, dwells the Lord. He alone is reality.

To truly know something, we must probe to its very essence. As the poet William Blake wrote:

To see a world in a grain of sand
And a Heaven in a wild flower,
Hold Infinity in the palm of your hand
And Eternity in an hour.

It is for this reason that the road is right in front of us. Whatever question we pursue whole-heartedly will bring us to the ultimate truth of life. Inactivity will not bring us towards our goal. Only when we begin to move do we discover the answer. The road, the path we must take, is directly in front of us: it is in an awareness of our lives, thoughts, actions and circumstances that we can discover the essence of life.

To make excuses as to why we cannot begin our journey towards Truth is to deny the simple fact that the road is before us. Jesus spoke of "each man taking up his cross and following me," this means accepting our lives, circum-stances and situations; taking responsibility and beginning our journey towards under-standing.

By beginning our journey to find Truth we are sure to succeed if we continue until our goal is won. Having a good guide will prove essential in this quest. Jesus said:

> *I am the light of the world; he who follows me shall not walk in darkness, but he shall find for himself the light of life.*
> —JOHN 8:12

Notice in this passage that Jesus says, ". . . he shall find for himself. . ." The seeker will find. Just because one decides to have a guide does not take away the responsibility of the seeker to tread the path towards Truth. Having taken the help of a guide does not diminish our achievement, rather, it only hastens it.

To quell our fears during our journey we seek solace in many ways: through escape, asceticism, philosophy, mountains, forests, shrines and graves. But the real solutions to our fears lie with a good guide. The Buddha, speaking 500 years before the birth of Jesus, said:

> *But that is not a safe refuge, [mountains, forests, shrines and graves] that is not the best refuge; a man is not delivered from all pains after having gone to that refuge.*
> *He who takes refuge in the Buddha, the Law and the Order; he who with clear under-*

*standing sees. . . having gone to that refuge,
a man is delivered from all suffering.*

—XIV: 189–192

These words are quite similar to those of Jesus,
uttered some 500 years later:

*Come to me, all who labor and carry burdens,
and I will give you rest.*

*Take my yoke upon you, and learn from
me, for I am gentle and meek in my heart, and
you will find rest for your souls.*

—MATTHEW 11: 28–29.

Lao Tzu describes the state of a true spiritual
teacher, one who firmly resides in the realm of
Truth:

*He who, conscious of his own light, is content
to be obscure,—he shall be the whole world's
model; his virtue will never fail. He reverts to
the Absolute.*

The Qur'an speaks of teachers and the guidance they offer:

*Muhammed is only a messenger; and many
a messenger has gone before him.*

A spiritual teacher is truly a messenger—he
or she stands as an intermediary between God

and humanity, relaying man's aspiration to God and God's Compassion and Blessings to man. The concept of a spiritual teacher being a messenger adds a feeling of humility to the role of a teacher. Humility abounds in a true teacher.

The road to understanding, to true knowledge, is right in front of us and a guide is waiting to help us. All we must do is take that first step, begin our journey, and all will be shown to us.

The first step undoubtedly requires great courage, but that courage is intensified if we have a guide to help us in our journey. The degree of our sincerity and determination will bring us a teacher of equal sincerity and understanding. As has been said, "When the student is ready, the teacher appears."

You have a multitude of questions.
But there is only one answer:
The road is right in front of you,
And the guide is waiting for you.

6

Spiritual Surrender

My Dubious Prayer-Life

My dubious prayer-life
May not satisfy God,
But my glowing surrender-heart
Will always satisfy God.

—SRI CHINMOY

Each of us wishes for many things in our lives. Each time we focus that hope or wish into a definite statement and ask that it be given to us it becomes a prayer.

A "dubious prayer-life," as Sri Chinmoy calls it, may refer to our endless parade of wants and desires. Life can, at times, be difficult and our prayers may seek solutions for those troubles. We may pray for others: that certain events will or will not happen to them. Regardless of the content of our prayer, we feel that our message is being heard by one who can grant our prayers: God.

Jesus enters the garden of Gethsemane and prays, ". . . Father, if it is possible, let this cup pass from me. . ." (Matthew 26:39). Jesus has become aware that he will be crucified and his first prayer is to ask that a different course of action take place.

Moments later, after finding his disciples sleeping, unable to keep watch for even one hour, Jesus again returns to pray: "Oh Father, if this cup cannot pass, and if I must drink it, let it be according to Thy Will."

This second prayer, "Let Thy Will be done," is nothing other than surrender. We often pray that things will turn out as we wish them to: that is our "dubious prayer-life." Our "glowing surrender-heart" appears the moment we let go of our own desires and accept the Will of God. After uttering the prayer, "Let Thy Will be done," there is nothing left to say. The mind is silent and the spiritual heart of acceptance comes forward.

Faith is a key element in spiritual surrender or acceptance. In the Bhagavad-Gita Sri Krishna speaks to Arjuna regarding a lack of faith:

But the man who is ignorant, who has no faith, who is of a doubting nature perishes. For the doubting soul, there is neither this world nor the world beyond nor any happiness.

—IV:40

As our faith grows we develop a trust in the creator of ourselves and the world. After praying, "Let Thy Will be done," we begin to listen for God's voice rather than dwell on our own wishes and desires. That listening is surrender to God's Will, and that, as Sri Chinmoy concludes his poem: "Will always satisfy God." Obviously, the Creator will be most satisfied when the creation, through a conscious decision, decides to trust in the Creator. Lao Tzu expresses this idea of surrender in a concise and powerful statement:

Do nothing by self-will, but rather conform to the Infinite Will, and everything will be done for you.

By conforming to the Infinite Will we are, in fact, surrendering ourselves to the essence and power of creation.

In the Muslim religion the concept of submission or surrender to God's will is a central theme which is discussed over and over in the Qur'an. "Islam" means surrender. The Qur'an:

*My service and sacrifice, my life and my
death, are all of them for God, the creator and
Lord of all the worlds.*

—6:162

By consciously trying to merge our will with
the Will of God, we begin the act of surrender.
This surrender is not a defeat or humiliation of
the weak by the strong, but rather the merging
of the finite with the infinite. The Qur'an says:

*Only he who surrenders to God with all his
heart and also does good, will find his reward
with his Lord, and will have no fear or regret.*

—2:112

As our will merges with that of the Creator we
become a more conscious participant in creation; we become conscious of the Creator. This
awareness is called God-realization or self-real-
ization which is the goal of all spiritual under-
takings: to unite our consciousness with the
consciousness of the Creator. The Katha
Upanishad describes this process:

*God, the Ancient and Eternal, is to be found
in the purification of the heart, in meditation,
in realization of the identify of the Self within
and Brahman without. Immortality is union
with God.*

Our surrender to God's Will is made possible through our awareness of God's Presence in all exsistence. The Old Testament sings the praise of God's omnipotence-hands:

Happy is he who has the God of Jacob for his help, whose hope is in the Lord his God, Who made heaven and earth, the sea and all that therein is; Who keeps truth forever; Who executes justice for the oppressed; Who gives food to the hungry. The Lord releases the prisoners; The Lord opens the eyes of the blind; the Lord raises those who are bowed down; the Lord loves the righteous; The Lord takes care of the poor; he feeds the fatherless and widows; but the way of the wicked he turns upside down.

PSALMS 146:5–9

*My dubious prayer-life
May not satisfy God,
But my glowing surrender-heart
Will always satisfy God.*

7

Two Universal Questions

Two Ancient Universal Questions

Two ancient universal questions:
How can I realise God
  Immediately?
Is unconditional surrender
  Ever possible?

—SRI CHINMOY

Thousands of years ago, Sri Krishna said to Arjuna:

But the yogi who strives with assiduity, cleansed
of all sins, perfecting himself through many
lives, then attains the highest goal.

—VI:45

The "highest goal" to which Sri Krishna refers is God-realization. All religions and spiritual philosophies have as their goal some type of conscious awareness of God.

To these ancient questions have been put forth a myriad of answers comprising the various methods of spiritual discipline. The various paths to God include learning, study, prayer, meditation, contemplation, correct attitude, work, action or any combination of these. Sri Krishna says:

> *. . . the path of knowledge for men of contemplation and that of works for men of action.*
>
> —III:3

Religious strife and conflict would be lessened if seekers had the simple understanding that: "Paths are many, Truth is one."

For the wise seeker the adverb "immediately," in Sri Chinmoy's poem is essential. To realize our conscious oneness with all of creation is no easy task. It is undoubtedly the most significant and challenging undertaking a person can attempt. There needs to be a sense of urgency concerning spirituality. Although we are seeking God, the eternal and immortal, we, as individuals, are severely limited by time. Our physical, conscious existence only lasts so long.

Whatever we wish to understand and experience must be achieved now while we are alive and conscious. Few know what lies beyond the gates of death. The Buddha, always direct and to the point said:

This body is wasted, frail, a nest of disease; this heap of corruption breaks to pieces, life indeed ends in death.

—XI:148

He continues offering a clue as to that which escapes the grip of death:

The brilliant chariots of kings wear away, the body likewise waxes old, but the virtue of good people knows not age

—XI:151

Therefore, in our striving for God-realization we must value time, our speed; our time frame is limited.

The poem concludes with the second question: "Is unconditional surrender ever possible?" This surrender is not the subjugation of a prisoner to a captor, but a oneness founded on wisdom and experience. If we are wise, we defer our judgement to those who know more than we do on a given subject. They are truly wise who surrender to the will behind all creation and existence.

Jesus made constant reference to the omnipotent power of God and the fact that his own actions came as a direct command from God:

For I did not speak of myself; but the Father who sent me, he commanded me what to say and what to speak.
—JOHN 12:49

Often we think that through surrender we are somehow limiting the range of our experience. This misconception is due to the fact that we forget the magnificent power and glory of the Source of all creation. Jesus speaks of the power of God:

This is why my Father loves me, because I lay down my life so that I may take it up again.
No man takes it away from me, but I lay it down of my own will. Therefore, I have the power to lay it down, and I have the power to take it up again. This command I received from my Father.
—JOHN 10:17–18

These powers to which Jesus has access come as a result of his surrender to God's Will: ". . . and I have the power to take it [life] up again." As our will merges with the will of the Infinite we come to know and experience a reality, power and peace far beyond any we can now imagine.

Yet, the question remains, "Is unconditional surrender ever possible?" The Isha Upanishad answers with a resounding "yes:"

They who devote themselves both to life in the world and to meditation, by life in the world overcome death, and by meditation achieve immortality.

What exactly is this state of meditation through which immortality can be achieved? The Katha Upanishad tells us:

When the senses stand still, when the mind and intellect do not move, that is called the highest state.

The same Upanishad also brings in the ideal of purity as an aspect of meditation:

. . . he who has understanding, who is mindful and always pure, reaches indeed the highest goal.

Spiritual teachers throughout the ages have taught that all seekers have the potential to achieve a conscious oneness with God. Jesus, in the Sermon on the Mount, proclaims:

*Blessed are the humble, for theirs is the king-
dom of heaven.*
  *Blessed are the pure in heart, for they shall
see God.*

—MATTHEW 5:8

Five hundred years earlier, the Buddha offered
out a similar teaching:

*But those who, when the Law has been well
preached to them, follow the Law, will reach
the further shore of the dominion of death,
hard to traverse though it be.*

Down through the ages prophets, saints and
sages have repeatedly answered "yes" to Sri
Chinmoy's question—Is unconditional surrender ever possible? Sri Chinmoy also offers a resounding "yes." He has written (Everest
Aspiration, p. 70):

*I am privileged that God has granted me a hu-
man incarnation. It is only in the human life
that I can realize Him, reveal Him and manifest Him unreservedly and unconditionally.*

Two ancient universal questions:
How can I realize God
Immediately?
Is unconditional surrender
Ever possible?

8

False Teachers

The Twentieth Century

The twentieth century
  Is flooded
With self-styled Master-rogues.
The twentieth century
  Is flooded
With monster disciple-fools.

—SRI CHINMOY

All sincere seekers need to pay careful attention
to this poem. The tragedies that have resulted
from "self-styled master-rogues" in our century
are well documented. Yet, as sincere seekers, we
realize that it is a great benefit in the spiritual

life to have a teacher who is living. Sri Krishna tells Arjuna:

> *Whenever there is a decline of righteousness and rise of unrighteousness, Arjuna, then I send forth myself.*
> *For the protection of the good, for the destruction of the wicked and for the establishment of righteousness, I come into being from age to age.*
>
> —IV:7–8

From "age to age" great spiritual teachers have come to help and guide humanity. How are we, as seekers, to know the true teachers from the false? Through careful observation and wise decisions we can steer ourselves clear of becoming "monster disciple-fools."

One way is through our own direct experience of the consciousness and realization of the teacher. This type of direct revelation of the teacher's true inner nature does take place, albeit, not often.

Not everyone is able to see the transfiguration of Jesus where ". . . his face shone like the sun, and his clothes turned white like light. And there appeared to them Moses and Elijah. . ." (Matthew 17:2–3). In the Bhagavad Gita Krishna reveals his universal form to Arjuna:

Wearing divine garlands and raiments, with divine perfumes and ointments, made up of all wonders, resplendent, boundless, with face turned everywhere.

If the light of a thousand suns were to blaze forth all at once in the sky, that night would resemble the splendor of that exalted Being.

There Arjuna beheld the whole universe, with its manifold divisions gathered together in one, in the body of the God of gods.

—XI:11–13

For those who are not blessed with such visions Jesus offers the following advice:

If I am not doing the works of my Father, do not believe me.

But if I am doing them, even though you do not believe in me, believe in the works, so that you may know and believe that my Father is with me and I am with my Father.

—JOHN 10:37–38

Therefore, if not through a direct experience of the teachers' realization, we can look and observe his or her actions. Krishna describes the purpose of his coming: "for the establishment of righteousness." The actions of any true master will, therefore, be in accord with establishing that which is good and loving upon earth. We need look no further than the lives of Buddha and Jesus to develop a standard by which to judge the lives and actions of other teachers who say they have access to the knowledge and wisdom of God.

Hindus regard the Vedas, of which the Upanishads are one section, as the highest spiritual authority. Any subsequent scripture or teacher, if they are to be regarded as valid, must be in agreement with the Vedas. A teacher may expand upon the teachings or develop them further, but never contradict them.

Jesus said, "I come not to destroy the scriptures, but to uphold them." A true spiritual teacher will have no part in any activity that does not promote that which is good, loving and in accordance with all of humanity's well-being.

Jesus wanted no part in hatred or violence:

. . . one of those who were with Jesus stretched out his hand and drew a sword, and struck it at the servant of the high priest, and cut off his ear.

Then Jesus said to him, Return the sword to its place; for all who take swords will die by swords.

—MATTHEW 26:51–52

By finding a genuine, living spiritual teacher, we can make tremendous spiritual progress. We can judge potential teachers through the following methods: a direct experience or vision of their realization; through their actions, and finally, through their adherence to that which you consider to be a true spiritual philosophy and morality.

Hypocracy cannot be accepted from a spiritual teacher. A teacher's actions must be in perfect accord with his or her teachings, and vice versa. Jesus criticized many of those with religious authority and power during his time:

Woe to you, scribes and Pharisees, hypocrites! For you are like tombs painted white, which look beautiful from the outside, but inside are full of dead bones and all kinds of corruption.

Even so, from the outside you appear to men to be righteous, but from within you are full of iniquity and hypocrisy.

—MATTHEW 23:27–28

There is an old saying: "When the student is ready, the teacher appears." We can make ourselves ready to receive a true spiritual teacher by cultivating sincerity, purity, simplicity and patience. These qualities will safeguard the seeker from false and misleading doctrines and teachers.

In Jesus' own time he foretold of the coming of false prophets saying:

And many false prophets will rise and will mislead a great many.
—MATTHEW 24:11

The Chandogya Upanishad also issues forth an alarming message for all seekers: "Whosoever follows a false doctrine of the Self will perish."

The Qur'an, a work of timeless wisdom which has guided the lives of millions of God-seekers, speaks on the issue of teachers and false gods:

There are happy tidings for those who keep away from the worship of false gods and turn to God in repetence. Give glad tidings to my creatures.

Those who listen to the Word and then follow the best it contains are the ones who have been guided by God, and are men of wisdom.
—39:17–18

In the twentieth century we find an abundance of "self-styled master-rogues," no doubt an indication of, in Sri Krishna's words: "a rise of unrighteousness." Let us not fall prey to these false teachers but keep our standard high, bearing in mind the examples of well-respected teachers from the past. Rather than "disciple-fools" let us make ourselves instruments of God's Will.

The twentieth century
  Is flooded
With self-styled Master-rogues.
The twentieth century
  Is flooded
With monster disciple fools.

9

Oneness in Multiplicity

My Heart's Constant Guest

My heart's constant guest:
God the Many.
My life's constant host:
God the One.

—SRI CHINMOY

This poem illustrates an idea that is central to spiritual philosophy, from the writings of Spinoza to the teachings of Buddha—God, although existing in the aspect of one Being, is also manifest in every aspect of creation. The Isha Upanishad says:

*In the heart of all things, of whatever there is
in the universe, dwells the Lord.*

Jesus, in his teachings, also offers forth this
idea. Already having proclaimed his oneness
with God, he goes on to say:

*For I was hungry, and you gave me food; I was
thirsty and you gave me drink; I was a
stranger and you took me in.*
    *. . . Truly I tell you, inasmuch as you have
done it to one of the least of these my brother,
you did it to me.*

—Matthew 25:35, 40

Jesus is clearly saying that God exists in each
one of us—in every aspect of creation. God exists in everyone.

God exists as one and in the multiplicity of
creation. Although God does exist in everything,
in some people that eternal energy shines more
brightly. This is especially true in the case of a
God-realized teacher such as Jesus or the Buddha. Jesus points this out to his disciples as they
scold a woman for anointing his head with precious perfume:

*When his disciples saw it, they were dis-
pleased, and said, why this waste?*

*For it could have been sold for a great sum,
and given to the poor.*
*But Jesus understood it and said to them,
Why are you troubling the woman? She has
done a good work for me.*
*For you always have the poor with you, but
you will not have me always.*
—MATTHEW 26:8–11

Jesus, although proclaiming the presence of God in all, does acknowledge the uniqueness of his own existence. Most people are unconscious of the eternal spirit within them. Those who are conscious of that depth and height are unique among humanity. Their words and actions ought to be given special notice. Each of us must aspire to manifest the greatest divinity we can perceive.

God, although existing in all, manifests most powerfully through the consciousness of a spiritual master. To be aware of and interact with such a teacher is one way to become more conscious of one's own inner resources.

This brings us to another important point illustrated by this poem. Some philosophies mistakenly assert that the world around us and those around us are nothing more than an illusion. It is said that only the Self, or soul, is real and all the physical reality is an illusion or *maya*.

Maya is a Sanskrit word which has mistakingly come to be defined as "illusion." Thus it is said, "the world is *maya,* or "illusion." By this line of reasoning many seekers have been mislead from the path of ultimate Truth. The fallacy is caused by a misunderstanding of the word *maya*. For a correct definition of this word let us turn to the words of Sri Krishna describing his existence in the world of multiplicity: "I come into being through my maya." (BG IV: 6) Clearly, *maya* is a power or force of creation and not an illusion, for God's powers are not an illusion. Furthermore, if we say that God is real, then all that He creates or exists within must be real. Jesus proclaims that he exists within each of us, including the poor and downtrodden. God then must also be within each of us. How can we call others' lives or experiences an illusion? If God exists as part and parcel of His creation then every experience we have is an experience which God has. By proclaiming the world an illusion we are only creating an excuse for not opening our hearts to "God the Many."

By calling the world and our experiences an illusion, we find a justification to disregard the commandment which Jesus proclaimed greater than all the rest: "A new commandment I give you, that you love one another, just as I have loved you." (John 14: 34). By calling the world an illusion, we are able to replace love with disregard and disinterest.

An awareness of "My life's constant host: God the One" is a powerful experience. Although we are many we find that all existence emerges from one source—that source is God. Different races, religions and civilizations may call God by different names and have different conceptions of God, but the undeniable fact is that we have all emerged from one God. The Prasna Upanishad illustrates this beautifully:

Man is composed of such elements as vital breath, deeds, thoughts, and the senses—all of them deriving their being from the Self [God]. They have come out of the Self, and in the Self they ultimately disappear—even as the waters of a river disappear in the sea.

That sea may be called many names: Brahma to a Hindu, Allah to a Moslem, the Father to a Christian, or Nirvana to a Buddhist; yet the various names simply describe a single source.

The Qur'an stresses again and again the presence of a single God—Allah—who is responsible for all of creation and existence.

Allah is God who created the heavens and the earth in six spans, then assumed His power, dispensing all affairs.

—10:3.

We may sense or feel God's Presence in many aspects of nature—the vast ocean, flowers, mountains and other people—yet behind these various manifestations exist a oneness. This unity is God.

God will, of course, continue to exist even though the creation may not. We have emerged from the source and will return to the source. In the opening lines of the Gospel of Saint John, we have a wonderful description of this:

The Word was in the beginning and that very Word was with God, and God was that Word.
The same was in the beginning with God.
Everything came to be by his hand and without him not even one thing that was created came to be.

—JOHN 1:1–3

According to the Upanishads "The Word" is "OM," and Brahman is the word used for God. Over 2000 years before the Gospel of St. John was written, the following passage was written in the Mundaka Upanishad:

The syllable OM, which is the imperishable Brahman, is the universe. Whatsoever has existed, whatsoever exists, whatsoever shall exist hereafter is OM. And whatsoever transcends past, present and future, that also is OM.

In this poem of Sri Chinmoy's, which transcends the narrow corridors of religious intol-
erance, we are called to accept God in two
aspects. These two aspects have been brought
to our attention by the Vedic Seers, Jesus and
many other spiritual teachers and sages.

My heart's constant guest:
God the Many.
My life's constant host:
God the One.

10

This Fleeting World

We Are Such Fools

*We are such fools
That we are seeking
    Permanence-joy
In a fleeting world.*

—SRI CHINMOY

Spiritual seekers in India often go and meditate on the flames of the funeral pyres at the cremation grounds. They do so to firmly fix in their minds the reality that nothing of this world lasts forever, not even our own body-existence.

There are three aspects of existence: creation, preservation and destruction. The world, that which we can experience and perceive through our senses, changes and all that we know eventually passes away. The empirical world is fleeting. Nothing remains or stays the same. All is in a constant state of flux and change.

Lao Tzu expresses this constant movement and change within life through simple, yet poignant, examples:

> *The course of things is such that what was in front is now behind; what was hot is now cold; what was strong is now weak; what was complete is now in ruin. Therefore, the Sage avoids excess, extravagance and grandeur.*

Lao Tzu, in the next passage, expresses the principle of creation, preservation and destruction. He also lays stress on the importance of understanding this reality in our lives:

> *All things alike do their work, and then we see them subside. When they have reached their bloom, each returns to its origin. Returning to their origin means rest or fulfillment of destiny. This reversion is an eternal law. To know that law is to be enlightened. Not to know it is misery and calamity.*

Sri Chinmoy's poem touches on one of the central truths that spiritual teachers throughout the ages have taught to their students: to expect permanence from this world will only lead to suffering, or, as Lao Tzu would say, "misery and calamity."

Assuredly, there are wonderful moments and experiences to be had from this life but "permanence-joy," as Sri Chinmoy expresses it, is not to be had from this realm of flux. There is joy and happiness but if it is dependent upon things of this world it cannot be permanent because that upon which it is based is not permanent. The Buddha said:

All existing things are transient. He who knows and sees this ceases to be in the thrall of grief.
　　　　　　　　　　　　　　　　　—XX:277

Suffering, sorrow and grief are caused by our inability to accept the fact that, in the end, nothing remains. The people we love, those things and possessions we earn and call "our own," our creations and. our achievements, even our memories and thoughts; all of these soon lose their form and dissolve into the mists of existence.

In the Katha Upanishad Nachikata, a seeker of Truth, in a dialogue with death, speaks the following truth:

I know that what is called a treasure is transient, for the eternal is not to be obtained in things which are not eternal.

The Qur'an also seeks to illumine the mind of the reader by differentiating between the transient and the eternal:

Know that the life of this world, it is nothing but a play and a pastime, an ornamentation, boasting and bragging among yourselves and multiplying in rivalry amost yourselves and lust for riches and children.

—57:20

The life of this world is only a sport and play. It is surely the home of the Hereafter that will be life extended and new, if only they knew.

—29:64

To base our happiness and well-being upon that which is ultimately fleeting means that there will come a time when there will be no foundation for our happiness and well-being. That is the moment when sorrows and sufferings begin. If "permanence-joy" is not to be found in this fleeting world, where can it be found, and equally important, what is "permanence-joy?"

"Permanence-joy" is a happiness founded upon that which never ceases. The Katha Upanishad speak of this awareness:

Fools follow the desires of the flesh and fall into the snare of all-encompassing death; but the wise, knowing the Self as eternal, seek not the things that pass away.

The "Self" referred to is none other than God. It is God alone who never ceases. Therefore, for a joy to last forever it would need to be founded upon an awareness of God. Jesus tells his disciples:

Beware of all covetousness, because life does not depend on abundance of wealth.

—LUKE 12:15

For Jesus there was only one goal in life worthy of struggle, and that was eternal life with the Father. He knew the fleeting things of this world would never satisfy our deep need for eternal joy:

. . . make for yourself purses which do not wear out, and a treasure in heaven that does not run short, where the thief does not come near, and moth does not destroy.

—LUKE 12:33

Jesus points to the soul of each of us as the dwelling place of that eternal aspect:

For how would a man be benefitted, if he should gain the whole world and lose his own soul.
—MATTHEW 16:26

If we are courageous enough to seek "permanence-joy," we come to realize, either through the sufferings and sorrows of life, or through wisdom, learning and meditation that this joy is to be found in God alone. The question then becomes one of utmost practicality: How do I attain God-realization? To answer that question we must study various spiritual teachings and teachers, find one to our liking and follow it wholeheartedly. Various teachers point towards different paths. Jesus offers some ideas which can help everyone in their search for Truth:

Love the Lord your God with all your heart and with all your soul and with all your might and with all your mind. This is the greatest and first commandment.
—MATTHEW 22:37–38

In the Mundaka Upanishad, it is said:

By the pure in heart He is known. The Self exists in man, within the lotus of the heart...

With mind illumined by the power of meditation, the wise know Him, the blissful, the immortal.

The Buddha offers another drop of that timeless wisdom from which all true teachers draw:

Those whose minds are well-grounded in the elements of knowledge, who rejoice in renunciation of affections and in freedom from attachment, whose evil propensities have been overcome and who are full of light, are completely liberated even in this world.

The greatest challenge each of us faces in our lives is finding that road which will lead us safely to our "permanence-joy." The realm of the eternal and immortal is not easy to find and yet, it is not so far away: The Mundaka Upanishad describes the journey well:

Brahman is supreme; he is self-luminous, he is beyond all thought. Subtler than the subtlest is he, farther than the farthest, nearer than the nearest. He resides in the lotus of the heart of every being.

To see the truth of this world—that all physical forms are indeed transient and fleeting—is one of the first steps in the search for the eter-

nal and everlasting. The Buddha, Christ or Sri
Chinmoy will all tell you that the empirical realm
is always shifting; modern physics will tell you
the same; but it is not until you actually feel and
experience this reality for yourself that you are
compelled to action. It is when we actually feel
the floor beneath us beginning to crumble that
we reach for something above us. When we tan-
gibly become aware that all we perceive with our
senses has no permanence we seek, and find as
quickly as possible, that which will not leave us.

We are such fools
That we are seeking
Permanence-joy
In a fleeting world.

11

Soul Power

You Cannot

You cannot
Change the world
With your mental thoughts.
  You can
Not only change the world
But also alter destiny
  If you invoke
Your inner cosmic energy
To come to the fore.

—SRI CHINMOY

Everyone reading this book is conscious of mental thoughts. Thoughts are constantly rising and falling in our minds. Our attention jumps from one thought to the next, often unceasingly, throughout the day and night.

We think of this, think of that, remember, plan, use thoughts constructively and to our own detriment. At any one time we can have thousands of potential thoughts. We plan, calculate, theorize, remember and imagine; all with thought. The undisciplined mind finds it difficult to stay with one thought or idea for any length of time. We jump from thought to thought giving no great power to any single thought. The people who are able to get something done in this world are those who can focus and concentrate on a single thought, emotion or idea with enough intensity and power to actually manifest that thought into a material form. To create anything in the material realm takes an intensification of thought energy. For most of us the mind drifts from thought to thought, giving no great intensity or power to any single thought or idea; therefore, our thoughts are ineffective instruments when it comes to creating change in the world. The Katha Upanishad reminds us of this fact:

He who lacks discrimination, whose mind is unsteady. . . never reaches the goal. . .

The Buddha taught the futility of undisciplined thought:

If a man's thoughts are unsteady, if he does not know the true law, his knowledge will never be perfect.

—III:38

The opposite of this wandering world of ceaseless thoughts is a mind that is single-pointed, focused and concentrated. Of this type of mind the Buddha also speaks:

As a fletcher makes straight his arrow, a wise man makes straight his trembling and unsteady thought, which is difficult to guard, difficult to hold back. . . a tamed mind brings happiness.

—III:33–35

The Katha Upanishad also tells us of the power of a focused mind:

When the five instruments of knowledge stand still together with the mind, and when the intellect does not move—this, say the wise, is the highest state.

What is it that will enable each of us to calm and focus our thoughts and awareness? Sri Chinmoy says this will happen when our "inner cosmic energy" comes to the fore. The energy of which he speaks is nothing other than our

soul-power, or the spirit of God within us. Jesus
called this energy faith and belief:

> *If you have faith and do not doubt, you will*
> *perform a deed not only like this of the fig tree,*
> *but should you say even to this mountain, Be*
> *removed and fall into the sea, it shall be done.*
> —MATTHEW 21: 21

The Qur'an also speaks of the importance of
faith and belief and how these qualities can af-
fect our lives:

> *Those who believe and find peace in their hearts*
> *from the contemplation of God: surely there is*
> *peace of heart in the contemplation of God.*
> *Those who believe and do the right, have*
> *happiness, and an excellent resting place.*
> —13:28–29

This power is something to which we all have
access. When Jesus' disciples were caught in a
storm at sea, Jesus appeared before them walking on the water. Peter was not sure if it was
Jesus, and, desiring proof said: "My Lord, if it is
you, command me to come to you on the water." The rest of the incident follows:

> *Jesus said to him, Come. So Peter went down*
> *from the boat and walked on the water, to*
> *come to Jesus.*

*But when he saw that the wind was strong,
he was afraid and began to sink, and he raised
his voice and said, My Lord, save me.*

*And the Lord immediately stretched out his
hand and grasped him; and he said to him,
Oh you of little faith, why did you doubt."*

—MATTHEW 15:29–31

In the vernacular of Jesus—when our faith, our "inner cosmic energy," has come to the fore we can do anything. Conversely, when that energy is not present, which Jesus calls a state of "doubt," we are literally "sunk."

This power is a real force which we can bring into our lives. It is tangible. As Jesus walked through a large crowd he was touched by a sick woman and she was healed.

*Jesus immediately knew that some power had
gone out of him; so he turned around to the
people and said, Who touched my garments?*

—MARK 5:30

This soul-power, when brought to the fore in our consciousness, immediately stills the mind and endows us with a great power and force, a power by which Peter could walk on water, a power by which we can, as Sri Chinmoy says: "change the world."

Beyond the realm of simply changing aspects of the world around us, Sri Chinmoy goes a step further and says that through this power we can "alter destiny." This is no small statement.

This energy for change comes from our soul, or the presence of God within us. The Katha Upanishad describes that power within us:

That being. . . dwells deep within the heart.
He is the lord of time, past and future.

Destiny is that which is ordained by the law of cause and effect. Every action and thought of ours will have an effect. That effect soon becomes the cause of further events, and so on, ad infinitum. Destiny, the law of cause and effect, operates within the structure of time. The Katha Upanishad tells us that the power deep within us is the "Lord of time, past and future." By learning to access our soul-power, we gain a deep awareness and understanding of time. We are then able to alter that which may have been destined. This ability to "alter destiny" ought not to be taken lightly. By accessing our "inner cosmic energy" we are harnessing the very power from which the whole structure of time emerges. That is how we are able to "alter destiny"—by no longer being bound by the confines of time's structure of past, present and future.

Through this "inner cosmic energy" we are able to change not only the physical reality but can also extend our power into the realm of spirit, creation, cause and effect.

Krishna tells Arjuna:

... a man of disciplined mind, who moves among the objects of sense, with the senses under control and free from attachment and aversion, he attains the purity of spirit.

—II:64

It is this "purity of spirit" that brings forth our true inner power.

We all know the futility of unfocused thought. It achieves no end, save a lazy pleasure. Krishna tells Arjuna:

... the thoughts of the irresolute are many-branched and endless.

—II:41

Following endless and many-branched corridors we are led only into a maze of unknowing and confusion. It is a futile journey, the journey without focus.

The other option we have, that of a focused and concentrated mind, fixed firmly upon our goals, will aid us towards finding and revealing our inner energy. With this energy firmly in our grasp, we can then move mountains and change the destiny of our lives and the lives of others. Lao Tzu describes this "inner cosmic energy:"

Without going out of doors, one may know the whole world; without looking out of the window, one may see the Way to Heaven. The further one travels, the less one may know. Thus it is that without moving you shall know, without looking you shall see, without doing you shall achieve.

Far from the ramblings of the restless, thought-ridden mind is the realm of our pure and sure soul-power. Through a steady and focused mind we can begin to feel this power in our hearts and lives.

You cannot
Change the world
With your mental thoughts.
    You can
Not only change the world
But also alter destiny
    If you invoke
Your inner cosmic energy
To come to the fore.

12

Self-Giving

No Partition
*There is neither a visible
Nor an invisible partition
Between self-giving
And God-becoming.*

—SRI CHINMOY

The goal of spiritual discipline, and the ultimate goal of life, is a conscious union with God and Truth. Either through conscious aspiration and an expanding awareness, or through the trials, tribulations, joys and sorrows of everyday experiences, we are either moving closer, or farther away, from an awareness of the unity of all existence. This movement towards God is our God-becoming.

Sri Chinmoy, in his poem, says that there is no difference between this process of God-becoming and actions of self-giving. An act of self-giving occurs when we give ourselves wholeheartedly and unconditionally to the service of others. Each time we put the needs of others above our own we are acknowledging an awareness of life and consciousness beyond our own limited ego. The very act of self-giving is a conscious movement towards an awareness of the oneness underlying the multiplicity of creation. The Mundaka Upanishad tells us:

The Lord is the Breath shining forth from all beings. Seeing him present in all, the wise man is humble, puts not himself forward, he becomes truly wise, not a talker only. His delight is in the Self, his joy is in the Self, he serves the Lord in all.

To see, experience and know God in every creature is a profound awareness. It is the experience of oneness. Lao Tzu expresses this awareness of oneness and the essence of self-giving as he describes the actions of a sage:

The Sage does not care to hoard. The more he uses for the benefit of others, the more he pos-

sesses himself. The more he gives to his fel-low-men, the more he has of his own.

The opposite of an act of self-giving is an act inspired by selfishness. The individual who acts from this motive is described by Lao Tzu:

He who is self-approving does not shine. He who boasts has no merit. He who exalts him-self does not rise. Judged according to Tao, he is like remnants of food or a tumor on the body—an object of universal disgust.

A feeling of oneness is a profound awareness. From this stems a humility, a humility that is in-finitely powerful, for it is based on a profound awareness of the God and spirit that moves through and sustains all of existence. True self-giving is founded upon this feeling.

Jesus stressed the power of humility. St. Mat-thew (5:3) quotes Jesus: "Blessed are the humble, for theirs is the kingdom of heaven." The humil-ity referred to is the humility of those who feel God in themselves and in others. When we feel that connectedness, we come to know that no one is any better or more important than an-other; we simply differ outwardly but within we are all manifestations of God.

Jesus, more so than many spiritual masters, put great importance on serving others:

For I was hungry and you gave me food; I was thirsty and you gave me drink; I was a stranger and you took me in.

. . . Truly I say to you, Inasmuch as you did not do it to one of these least ones, you also did not do it to me.
—MATTHEW 25:35, 44

To love another person unconditionally is a wonderful feeling of oneness and acceptance. To offer service to that person is doubly powerful for we are passing beyond the realm of feeling and emotion and into the realm of action and manifestation.

True self-giving is founded upon a realization of oneness and not upon pride: the belief that we are better than others and they need our help. If we think that we are cast from a finer mold, or more important than others, we are making a big mistake. Those who are the rich and powerful of this world often think they are better, more significant and more important that others in God's Creation. It is due to this type of pride that Jesus said:

Truly I say to you, It is difficult for a rich man to enter into the kingdom of heaven.
—MATTHEW 19:23

When we leave this world, we leave all material possessions behind. Therefore, it is not the physical bulk of riches that holds the rich back from heaven, but rather it is the weight of the pride which most often accompanies those riches. As one becomes more enamored with the pleasures and powers of this earthly realm, it becomes increasingly difficult to shift ones awareness into the spiritual essences of existence. By increasing the weight of our own ego-importance, we are forgetting the reality of oneness pulsing through all of creation. We may gain the world, yet in the process we lose our soul.

Actions that are based on pride create a heavy weight. We often act so that we may acquire. From the possession of that which we acquire we feel that we will find happiness; we may find though that our possessions simply serve to strengthen our pride, which does not bring true, lasting happiness, for only happiness that is based on oneness will outlast the flux of the material world.

Conversely, when we serve others—self-giving—we expand our awareness of God in all. The Isha Upanishad says:

To the illumined soul, the Self is all. For him who seeks everywhere oneness, how can there be grief or delusion?

To act upon this feeling of oneness serves to strengthen our awareness of oneness.

Sri Chinmoy, who emphasizes self-giving as one of the essential ingredients in the spiritual life, has said that an hour of unconditional self-giving is equal to an hour of the highest meditation. Jesus told his disciples:

If you wish to be perfect, go and sell your possessions and give them to the poor, and you will have a treasure in heaven; then follow me.

—MATTHEW 19:21

The treasure to which Jesus refers is nothing other than an awareness of God in all. Sacrifice is one of the most powerful expressions of love. Self-giving is a form of sacrifice. In a moment of pure self-giving we put our self, or ego, the little "I," in a place of secondary importance and apply our awareness to the needs of those we are acting for.

The Qur'an echoes the words of Jesus and other teachers who stress the importance of true self giving:

. . . and do not forget your part in this world. Do good to others as Allah has done good to you.

—28:77

And those saved from the covetousness of their own souls—they are the ones that achieve prosperity.

—59:9

Piety lies in believing in God. . . and disbursing your wealth out of love for God among your kin and orphans, the wayfarers and mendicants. . .

—2:177

To see God in the depths of our meditation is indeed a powerful experience. To see God in all that exists is a still higher experience. To serve God in all is the highest experience.

If our actions are stemming from humility and love then our self-giving will be unconditional: free from any expectation regarding result or outcome. Krishna says to Arjuna:

Thou hast a right to action, but only to action, never to its fruits; let not the fruits of thy works be thy motive. . .

—II:47

All that we can do is act based upon what we observe, think and feel. If we have a pure heart and humility, our actions will stem from a feeling of oneness. Once we have acted the results will come as they may. We did not create the universe or those beings within it. Once we have acted we must place our actions devotedly at the feet of God. Why things happen as they do is often far beyond our realm of understanding. If we expect a certain result from our actions we will often be frustrated, for few of us can fully comprehend life's mysteries and movements. Krishna offers Arjuna further advice regarding action:

> *He who abandons all desires and acts free from longing, without any sense of mineness or egotism, he attains the great peace.*
>
> —II:71

As we leave behind expectation we come to know peace.

Action and movement are essential for the continuation and growth of life. Since we are compelled by life to act, let us have as the basis of our actions a feeling of love and humility based on oneness. Each of our actions can be coupled with the prayer, "Let thy will be done." This simple utterance will allow us to offer up the fruits of our actions to the Creator of all existence.

Freed from the snare of expectation we are bound to experience our God-becoming.

> *There is neither a visible*
> *Nor an invisible partition*
> *Between self-giving*
> *And God-becoming.*

13

Success

Only Those Will Be Successful
Only those will be successful
  In the spiritual life
Who have the indomitable courage
To face their life-problem-challenges.

—SRI CHINMOY

Arjuna, a spiritual seeker and warrior, stands amidst a great battle. He has a problem. He must decide whether or not to fight. The potential enemy are the doers of evil deeds yet they are family and old friends of Arjuna. To walk away from the entire situation is an option. His teacher and friend, Krishna, stands by his side. Krishna is prepared to confront the challenge. He knows the supreme truth that difficulties must be faced and overcome. To the despondency and confusion of Arjuna, Krishna says:

> *Yield not to this unmanliness, Arjuna, for it does not become thee. Cast off this petty faint-heartedness and arise. . .*
> —II:3

Krishna compels his student to arise and confront the challenge of understanding the nature of the problem he faces and then act according to the knowledge therein gained.

Success in any endeavor depends upon growth. Growth is change. Every change requires a rearrangement of whatever medium we are working with or in. Change requires some type of action. Most people call the need for change by another name: a problem. Wiser people call the same change, a need for change, a challenge. Sri Chinmoy, in his poem, accepts both vantage points, and in an effort to get his message across, calls these happenings: "life-problem-challenges."

Whatever we choose to call these moments when change is necessary, one thing is sure: we need to take some type of action. Certain emotions may prevent us from acting: fear, self-doubt, insecurity and jealousy. Krishna says:

". . . cast off this petty faintheartedness." We must rise to the occasion. To face a great challenge we need to muster up faith, courage and other qualities and then act.

Doubt, insecurity and a lack of self-confidence lessen our ability to act with effectiveness. These emotions and negative thoughts will destroy our courage and determination. Jesus tells us:

Every kingdom which is divided against itself will be destroyed; and every house or city that is divided against itself will not stand.
—MATTHEW 12:25

If we divide ourselves by these negative thoughts we will not be able to act effectively. We will not be able to cultivate an "indomitable courage."

All too often spirituality is seen as a departure from the world, as an attempt to leave behind our day-to-day problems and difficulties and retreat into peace. Unfortunately, that escape from the world is not the ultimate peace which a true seeker can experience. The Buddha taught:

Men driven by fear go to many a refuge, to mountains and forests, to shrines and graves and sacred trees.

But that is not safe refuge, that is not the best refuge; a man is not delivered from all pains after having gone to that refuge.

He who takes refuge with Buddha, the Law and the Order; he who with clear understanding sees the four noble truths. . .

That is the safe refuge, that is the best refuge.

—XIV:188–192

This "safe refuge" is an inner wisdom and understanding that is not reached through escape, but only through powerful, soulful action, learning and growth. The Qur'an also speaks of taking refuge in a belief and knowledge of a higher power or force at play in our lives:

. . . say when assailed by adversity: "Surely we are for Allah, and to Him we shall return."

—2:156

The "clear understanding" of which the Buddha speaks is developed through spiritual discipline, prayer and meditation, not by retreating from life's problems and difficulties.

In facing problems and difficulties we must utilize our deepest power and strength. This strength arises from our soul. Lao Tzu describes aspects of this inner strength:

I have three precious things which I hold fast and prize. The first is gentleness; the second is frugality; the third is humility, which keeps me from putting myself before others. Be gentle, and you can be bold; be frugal, and you can be liberal; avoid putting yourself before others, and you can become a leader among men.

"Indomitable courage" is essential for facing life's challenges. Where will this courage come from?

We can find many sources of courage: our family, friends, those we love, certain ideals we hold, our past experiences, and our hopes and dreams. Ultimately, the source of all courage is love and oneness. The Taittiriya Upanishad tells us the cause of fear, the opposite of courage:

So long as there is the least idea of separation, there is fear.

Put in the affirmative, we could say that where there is oneness, there is no fear. Where there is no fear, we find boundless courage.

Jesus had only three years to teach and prepare his disciples to spread the truths he had realized throughout the world. He knew they would face great difficulties and challenges. Preparing them for these difficulties he said:

This is my commandment: that you love one another just as I have loved you.

*There is no greater love than this—that a man
lay down his life for the sake of his friends.*

Jesus, who preached a gospel of love, is saying that love can be strong enough so that we
can face even our own death by summoning
forth this feeling of love and oneness.

It is only through love that we go beyond our
sense of ego: me being separate from you. To lay
down one's life for another is to feel that his or
her existence is equally significant to our own.
When we experience that feeling we are step-
ping beyond our small ego-world and into a vast
oneness-world.

In life we have many problems and challenges
to face. How we face those situations will greatly
influence the quality of our lives. Cultivating a
courage based on love and oneness will give us
the inner strength to effectively face these "life-
problem-challenges." In life we experience
many moments that require change and growth.
With courage founded upon love and oneness
we can face all of these challenges.

*Only those will be successful
    In the spiritual life
Who have the indomitable courage
To face their life-problem-challenges.*

14

A Mind of Peace

How Can We Expect

*How can we expect
To make our mind peaceful
And our heart blissful
If we do not keep God
As the center of our attention
  All the time?*

—SRI CHINMOY

There can be no greater joy than to consciously merge with the source of all creation. Think of how much you love something you have created: a painting, poem, house, friendship or other things and events into which you have put your valuable time and energy. Now try to imagine the love that the Creator must have for us, the creation. We can search for God and Truth in many ways and in many places. The Mundaka Upanishad offers for us some advice in that quest:

The Self cannot be gained through the study of the scriptures, nor by the subtlety of understanding, nor through much learning. But by him who longs for Him is He known.

All of us, through our multifarious activities and desires, are ultimately seeking a peaceful mind and a loving heart. We all know the feeling of frustration, depression, self doubt and nervousness—they torment our minds. Peace feels so much better.

We know the feeling of a broken heart, or a heart torn in different directions. A feeling of love and bliss in our hearts is much sweeter and satisfying.

If we wish to make peace and love permanent experiences in our lives, then it is imperative to experience and cultivate these feelings and to also find the source of these wonderful emotions.

We often associate certain events, people or experiences with feelings of love and peace. We once did something and while doing it, or afterwards, felt peace of mind. Mistakenly, we assume that the peace exists independent of the event or situation, when, in reality, the peace came from our soul or from God. The Brihadaranyaka Upanishad makes this clear:

The world existed first as seed, which as it grew and developed took on names and forms. As a razor in its case or as fire in wood, so dwells the Self, the Lord or the universe, in all forms even to the tips of the fingers. Yet the ignorant do not know him, for behind the names and the forms he remains hidden.

If we are wise, we will seek the source of peace and love if we wish to make them a regular part of our awareness and existence. A genuine spiritual teacher always points the disciple to the Source. Jesus taught his disciples:

Love the Lord your God with all your heart and with all your soul and with all your might and with all your mind.
This is the greatest and the first commandment.

—MATTHEW 23:37–38

Jesus, who was teaching his students to reach the consciousness and awareness of the eternal, taught his followers that by loving God, and thinking about God, one will find eternal bliss.

The Buddha, who also taught seekers a path to deep and abiding peace once said:

The disciples of Gotama [the Buddha] are always wide awake and watchful, and their thoughts day and night are ever set on the Buddha.

—XXI:296

Again, we find the teacher pointing to a focus on God as the surest way to find the source of peace and bliss. Each time we turn away from that source, or lose our awareness of God, we are missing an opportunity to commune with the source of creation.

Jesus, well aware of the difficulties, troubles and worries of daily living, was nevertheless adamant that focusing on God was the essential aspect of living. In beautiful words he explains:

Therefore, do not worry or say, What will we eat, or what will we drink, or with what will we be clothed?

For worldly people seek after all of these things. Your Father in heaven knows that all of these things are also necessary for you.

But seek first the kingdom of God and his righteousness, and all these things shall be added to you.

*Therefore, do not worry about tomorrow;
for tomorrow will look after itself. Sufficient
for each day is its own trouble.*

—MATTHEW 6:31–34

We face the same basic worries and difficulties today as people did in the time of Jesus: the acquisition of food, shelter and clothing. The message of Jesus applies just as much today as it did 2000 years ago: focus on God and love first; God will care for his creation; do not worry.

The God to which great spiritual teachers tell us to turn our attention is not the God of men's minds. Our minds can never grasp the immensity of God. Unfortunately, some teachers and philosophers have tried to define God in mental, concrete terms and therefore the conceptions relayed to most people fall light years short of the Beauty, Power and Love that is God. Consequently, many people become disenchanted with the word God and any teachings espousing the idea of God.

Great spiritual teachers, unlike those who try to manipulate others through certain conceptions of God, teach and speak of God in a way that is wondrous and appealing. In the Chandogya Upanishad we find God described as Light:

The light that shines above the heavens and above this world, the light that shines in the highest world, beyond which there are no others—that is the light that shines in the hearts of men.

This is a presentation of God which is warm, appealing and open to each individual's needs and aspirations. God is not only in the highest heavens, he or she is also within each one of us.

Jesus gave up his own life to fulfill the wish of his Father. After becoming aware of his possible crucification he prayed:

Oh my Father, if this cup cannot pass, and if I must drink it let it be according to thy will.
—MATTHEW 26:42

Each of us, depending on our vantage point, will have a different conception of who or what God is. Masculine or feminine, just or merciful, peaceful or powerful—many are the ways to conceive of God. God has infinite attributes and depending on who we are and where we are in our lives we will perceive a different aspect. Many people can stand on the seashore watching the sun set. Each perceives the light reflecting in the water coming directly to them. So, too, we each see God differently according to where we stand. No one can tell you who or what God is, for God is different to all.

The Brihadaranyaka Upanishad gives an analogy of God and life comparing existence to a wheel:

> *The Self is the land of all beings, the king of all beings. And as all spokes are contained in the axle and in the felly of a wheel, all beings, all creatures, all gods, all worlds, all lives are contained in the Self.*

True spiritual teachers never force a certain conception of God upon the student, but rather encourage the seeker to try to see God in whatever way appeals to the seeker. We must think of God and meditate on God in a way that resonates with our individuality. Some conceive of God in the personal form, others choose a form embodying infinite intelligence or emotion.

As seekers of abiding peace and love we find ourselves drawn to the source of these feelings. The Qur'an tells us upon which road we are most likely to find peace and happiness:

> *The true way with God is peace. . .*
>
> —3:19

Once we find this source we must put as much of our awareness in that direction as possible if we are to truly connect with the vastness and potential that is ourselves, that is God.

The pious men of old used to wait an hour in silent meditation and then offer their prayer, in order to direct their heart to their Father in heaven.

MISHNAH, BERACHOTH, V, 1

How can we expect
To make our mind peaceful
And our heart blissful
If we do not keep God
As the center of our attention
   All the time?

15

Innocence, Purity, and Sincerity

What You Need

*What you need
Is a life of innocence.
What you need
Is a heart of purity.
What you need
Is a mind of sincerity.
Do you need anything else
To realize God?
No! This is enough,
More than enough.*

—SRI CHINMOY

To realize and become consciously aware of the source of all existence—God—is a vast undertaking and a lofty, difficult achievement. Some say that an awareness of God is the ultimate goal of life. The desire to know the source of our creation is a natural and spontaneous act. Because of the immensity of the journey, most people never completely reach the goal, although some do. Those who do and then choose to return to the day-to-day world to help others in the same pursuit are called spiritual teachers.

Once we have found a teacher it is natural to ask: What exactly do I need in order to reach the goal, an awareness of God? As we look down the corridors of time we find many great spiritual teachers echoing the words of Sri Chinmoy, or, he echoing theirs.

The poem first calls for "a life of innocence." When we think of innocence we often think of children. Jesus says:

See to it that you do not despise one of these little ones; for I say to you, their angels always see the face of my Father in heaven.

—MATTHEW 18:10

He also says:

Truly I say to you, unless you change and become like little children, you shall not enter the kingdom of heaven.

—MATTHEW 18:3

These passages give us an intuitive feeling for innocence. A life of innocence is a life of goodness and right action. The Buddha offered the following advice:

Do not follow the evil law! Do not live of thoughtlessness! Do not follow false doctrines! . . .

Rouse thyself! Do not be idle! Follow the path of righteousness and shun transgression. The righteous man rests in bliss, in this world and in the next.

—XIII:167–168

Deep within, with the help of our conscience, we know right from wrong. A life of innocence follows the path that stems from the sweet, innocent eyes of a child.

The poem then calls for a "a heart of purity." Our spiritual heart is the core of our being. In describing the spiritual heart Jesus says:

For where your treasure is, there also will be your heart.

—LUKE 12:34

The awareness of the spiritual heart is deeper than the realm of thought. Within our spiritual heart are our deepest feelings and desires, those select things and feelings around which our life revolves. The Katha Upanishad describes the danger of an impure heart:

He who lacks discrimination, who is mindful and always impure never reaches the goal.

Jesus put this in the affirmative during his Sermon on the Mount:

Blessed are the pure in heart, for they shall see God.
—MATTHEW 6:8

Jesus, speaking to his disciples, described those who did not understand his teachings:

Because to you it is granted to know the mystery, but it is not granted to them.
For the heart of this people has become hardened, and they hear with difficulty, and their eyes are dull; so that they cannot see with their eyes and hear with their ears and understand with their hearts...
—MATTHEW 13:11,15

From this passage we see that spiritual understanding takes place within the heart. A spiritual heart that has become "hardened," cannot feel God or know Truth. A pure heart is open to the subtle vibration of spirituality and has not become overwhelmed by the desires of coarse material sensations. Most people lose their purity of heart as they seek happiness in the world of objects and possession. Jesus warns of the pitfalls of material pursuits:

> *For how can a man be benefitted if he gain the whole world, but lose his own soul, or even weakens it?*
>
> —LUKE 9:25

To keep our hearts pure we must stay attuned and aware of the finer and more subtle energies which exist in life such as love, compassion, oneness and forgiveness. All of these exist within a heart of purity.

Lastly, the poem points to "a mind of sincerity." Within a pure heart there is abundant sincerity. The challenge is to bring that sincerity into our day-to-day thought world. Sincerity allows for a pure expression of our thoughts and emotions.

To be insincere is to be dishonest, manipulative and hypocritical. To create sincerity within ourselves is to open a channel for the expression of our deep, heart-felt emotions. Sincerity knows how to express Truth. Sincerity is developed through the practice of honesty and integrity—these qualities are stressed in the practice of Buddhism. Sincerity is a very real power. In the words of the Buddha:

The young monk who applies himself to Buddha's teachings, lights up this world like the moon freed from clouds.

—XXV:382

Sincerity can have a real force and power in this world. As our sincerity grows we come closer and closer to our own deepest feelings and we are able to project these feelings to the world around us.

The poem then asks if there is anything else needed in order to realize God. This is a significant question because the three qualities or attributes so far mentioned, although surely a challenge, are within the grasp of each of us. The answer given in the poem is, "No." All we need to realize God is sincerity in our mind, purity in our hearts and an innocence in our life.

Worldly achievements: money, name and fame, are not mentioned as necessary to reach God. In fact, Jesus, when approached by one who wished to follow him, said:

If you wish to be perfect, go and sell your possessions and give them to the poor and you will have a treasure in heaven; then follow me.

—MATTHEW 19:21

Unfortunately, in this day and age, money is sometimes put forward as an important ingredient and aspect of spiritual growth. Many churches and religious organizations have amassed great wealth. Few who have read the gospels can forget the words of Jesus as he entered the temple:

And Jesus entered into the temple of God, and drove out all who were buying and selling in the temple, and he overturned the trays of the money changers and the stands of those who sold doves.

And he said to them, It is written, my house shall be called the house of prayers; but you have made it a bandit's cave.

—MATTHEW 21:12–13

Just as an individual needs to have a pure heart to feel God's touch, so too, any organization offering spirituality to people must be pure and follow the same spiritual guidelines offered to individual seekers.

Ornate temples and displays of power do not bring God any closer to man. God, according to the great spiritual teachers, is drawn to us by sincere prayers and sublime meditations.

Achieving various mystical states or accumulating certain types of knowledge—such as magical words or secret scriptures—are also not mentioned as necessary to reach God. The essential truth being expressed in this poem is that no one holds a special key to heaven that can be sold or given to another. There are no valuable, secret truths or teachings to which a chosen few have access. In order to uphold various so-called religious or spiritual structures, certain people are put forward as having special knowledge or access to God. For a genuine seeker to fall into this type of belief system is a real tragedy. The Mundaka Upanishad sheds light on the truth that all have access to God:

> *By the pure in heart is He known. The Self exists in man, within the lotus of the heart and is the master of his life and his body. The wise who understand this behold the Immortal which shines forth full of bliss.*

Again, we find no mention of material wealth or secret scriptures. Rather, we are once again called to cultivate a purity in our hearts and to make our minds clear, sincere and strong through the practice of meditation. We find no mention of the need for any type of hierarchy or large, powerful organizations to bring to us the knowledge of God.

Down through the ages genuine spiritual teachers have been guiding men and women towards a special awareness, the keys to which are within each one of us, here and now.

What you need
Is a life of innocence.
What you need
Is a heart of purity.
What you need
Is a mind of sincerity.
Do you need anything else
To realize God?
No! This is enough,
More than enough.

16

Philosophy, Religion, and Spirituality

Philosophy Embodies

*Philosophy embodies
   God-information.
Religion embodies
   God-aspiration.
Spirituality embodies
   God-satisfaction.*

—SRI CHINMOY

Philosophy, religion and spirituality. Anyone seeking answers to the deepest questions in

life—Who am I?; Who or what created my existence?; What is the purpose of existence?—will
eventually walk along one, or all, of these three
roads: philosophy, religion and spirituality.

Philosophy is a science. The central instrument used in the quest for knowledge and understanding is the reasoning, analytical, logical
mind. We use philosophy to create a world-view
with which we can make sense out of a world
which, in reality, we know very little. We gather
information from the world we sense around us
and the experiences we have; from there we
build a philosophy, a way of seeing ourselves and
life. Philosophies can vary because individuals,
their environments, and their experiences are
often quite different. Our mind, the main instrument for inquiry, is greatly influenced by environment.

It is interesting to note that existential philosophy had among its greater proponents men
and women who had lived in German-occupied
Paris during World War II. Jean Paul Satre wit-
nessed Jews being forced into railway cars
bound for concentration camps.

The author of *Waiting for Godot,* Samuel
Beckett, sat watching the same scene. The ob-
servations and information those individuals
were taking in during that time became the basis of existentialism. Because the information

gathered in philosophic inquiry is limited to what is observable with the mind and senses, there are inherent limits to philosophy. In the course of time, one philosophy is replaced by the next. Human beings change as does our environment. Philosophy's significance is that it is the first step in the exploration of existence, in that it sharpens one's mind and intellect. In any search, we must begin by gathering information. In the science of philosophy, we gather information about humankind, morals, ethics, and all that we can perceive of life.

Interestingly, as we push our minds farther and farther into the mysteries of life, we begin to perceive the limits of the mind. The collection of information can take us only so far. For the mind to perceive more and more it must be made more silent, still and subtle.

Lao Tzu illustrates the difference between book learning and the experience stemming from a deep silence within ourselves. This silence emerges as our mind becomes silent and still. He describes this as a state of inaction:

The pursuit of book learning brings about daily increase. The practice of Tao brings about daily loss. Repeat this loss again and again, and you arrive at inaction. Practice inaction and there is nothing which cannot be done.

The loss he describes is the loss of the ever-active mind. The practice of Tao is an awareness of the natural way of existence, which we can experience when we have the profound awareness created by a silent mind. When we enter the stillness of the mind we find that life resonates deeply within us. This feeling awakens our spiritual heart. Our heart longs for a reconnection with the essence of life.

Aspiration, a term used by Sri Chinmoy and other spiritual teachers, is a heart-felt desire to know, see and understand the mysteries of existence. The spiritual heart and a deep longing to know God replaces philosophy's inquisitive mental search. Heart replaces mind as the primary instrument of search. This is where a religious search begins.

Any search requires sacrifice. If we are to travel quickly, we must lighten our load. Religion helps us to do this by presenting the seeker with guidelines for spiritual understanding. When Jesus preached his Sermon on the Mount he offered seekers inner challenges that, if met, would bring them closer to God:

> *Blessed are the pure in heart, for they shall see God.*
> *Blessed are the peacemakers, for they shall be called sons of God.*

*Let your light so shine before men that
they may see your good works and glorify
your Father in heaven.*

—MATTHEW 5:8,9,16

Religion offers guidelines for the seeker and a
structure through which to seek God. A religion
is a home, a structure, which gives us a comfort
while we seek Truth. Religions also often offer
the comfort of some type of reward if we live our
lives to a certain code. In the Taittiriya Upanishad we find the essence of the moral code
upon which religions are founded:

*Say what is true. Do your duty. Do not ne-
glect the study of the scriptures. Do not cut
the thread of progeny. Do not swerve from
the truth. Do not swerve from duty. Devi-
ate not from the path of good. Revere great-
ness.*

We are offered guidelines by which to live and
are also promised certain rewards if these actions are performed. In the Chandogya
Upanishad it is written:

*In like manner, whosoever among mortals
knows the Self, meditates upon it, and re-
alizes it—he too obtains all the worlds and
all desires.*

The Qur'an also promises a reward for those who adhere to its guidelines for thought and action:

If any do deeds of righteousness—be they male or female—and have faith, they will enter Heaven and not the least injustice will be done to them.

—4:124

For those who do good things there is goodness and more, and not blot or disgrace will cover their faces. They are people of Paradise, where they will abide forever.

—10:26

Religion offers a system with which we can feel comfortable, and since different seekers have different tendencies, there should be many religions, for all true religions are ultimately going to the same place—God. If our aspiration is intense enough, we will be willing to make certain changes in our lives and discipline ourselves in order to find that which we are seeking: God. The seeker's final step in the quest for God and Truth is the step into pure spirituality.

Spirituality is the individual's journey into the unknown. Rules, codes of conduct and the promise of certain rewards and gains must now be left behind to begin the true journey into consciousness that goes far beyond the realm of thoughts and ideas. The Mundaka Upanishad describes this next step:

> *The Self is not to be known through study of the scriptures, nor through subtlety of the intellect, nor through much learning. But by him who longs for him is he known. Verily unto him does the Self reveal his true being.*

The passage suggests that, in the end, what brings us to God is our deep, heart-felt longing and nothing else. It is a longing for which we are willing to sacrifice all else. A handful of individuals had the courage to love Jesus. He, being a true teacher, knew the great journey that awaited them and the necessary sacrifice. Matthew describes the sacrifice:

> *And while he was walking by the sea of Galilee he saw two brothers. . . who were casting nets into the sea, for they were fishermen.*
>
> *And Jesus said to them, follow after me and I will make you become fishers of men.*
>
> *So they immediately left their nets and followed him.*
>
> —MATTHEW 5:18–20

Jesus, the teacher, challenged them with a radical change. He asked them to leave all that had been theirs and accept an entirely new life—a life of spirit.

If we equate religion with a house, we could say that spirituality is the road which many houses share. Eventually, we must all emerge from our different homes and journey along the road which we all have in common. At that time, we leave behind the comforts of home and embark upon the path of spirituality.

A journey into the realm of spirit and consciousness is no easy task. Jesus stressed faith as a key element in the journey:

If there is faith in you even as a grain of mustard seed, you will say to this mountain, move away from here, and it will move away; and nothing would prevail over you.

—Matthew 17:20

This depth of faith is something we can all access. Jesus tells a woman, who had touched his cloak and been healed of twelve years of hemorrhage:

Have courage, my daughter, your faith has healed you. . .

—Matthew 9:22

Jesus goes on to say that this type of faith can be acquired through intense, deep prayer. In the Chandogya Upanishad, written thousands of years earlier, we find the same advice:

. . . all shall be yours if we but dive deep within.

The journey of spirituality is not easy. The Buddha said:

Few are there among men who arrive at the other shore; the other people here merely run up and down the shore.

—VI:85

With courage, faith, prayer and meditation it is possible to reach an awareness of God. The poem ends with the line: "Spirituality embodies God-satisfaction." God's satisfaction surely dawns each time a part of creation consciously merges with the whole. The Buddha says of those who merge with the Eternal:

Good people shine from afar, like the peaks of Himalay; bad people are not seen here, like arrows shot by night.

—XXI:304

Jesus pointed to a flower in order to teach the wonderment of life:

*Observe the flowers, how they grow; for they
do not toil nor do they spend; but I say to you
that not even Solomon in all his glory was
arrayed like one of these.*

—LUKE 12:27

If Creation put such beauty into a flower, what
wonderment must be within the hearts and
souls of each one of us? That is the goal of spirituality: each individual's journey into the core
of existence. Spirituality is based upon direct
experience, not the ideas or theories of others.
Jesus says:

*Truly, truly, I say to you, We speak only what
we know, and we testify only to what we have
seen. . .*

—JOHN 4:11

The individual who reaches beyond thoughts
and ideas and into the realm of consciousness
through direct experience is exploring true
spirituality. This is the realm of existence, consciousness, love and oneness—a realm that
must be experienced directly and can never be
known through mere words and study. It is a
realm that transcends our daily, fleeting experiences, yet also encompasses them. In spirituality exists God-satisfaction.

Philosophy embodies
God-information.
Religion embodies
God-aspiration.
Spirituality embodies
God-satisfaction.

To everything there is a season, and a time for every purpose under the sun: A time to be born and a time to die; a time to plant and a time to pluck up that which is planted; A time to kill and a time to heal; a time to tear down and a time to build up; A time to weep and a time to laugh; a time to mourn and a time to dance; A time to cast away stones and a time to gather stones together; a time to embrace and a time to refrain from embracing; A time to lose and a time to seek; a time to tie up and a time to untie; A time to rend and a time sew; a time to keep silent and a time speak; A time to love and a time to hate; a time for war and a time for peace. What profit has the worker in his labor? I have seen the toil which the Lord has given to the sons of men to be engaged therewith. He has made everything beautiful in its time; also he has made the world dear to man's heart, so that no man can find out the works which the Lord has done from the beginning to the end. I know that there is no good in worldly things, but for men to rejoice and to do good in their lives. And also that every man should eat and drink and enjoy the good of all his labor; it is the gift of the Lord. I know that whatsoever the Lord does, it shall be for ever; nothing can be added to it and nothing taken away from it; and the Lord has so made it that men should reverence him. That which is now, already has been; and that which is to be, has already been; and God will avenge him who has been persecuted.

ECCLESIASTES 3:1–15

17

Decisions

At Every Moment

At every moment
We have to decide
Whether we want
The division-desiring mind
Or the union-aspiring heart.

—SRI CHINMOY

Mankind, no longer entirely bound by nature's unconscious commands, is able to make conscious decisions, to act according to free will. At any given moment we can turn our attention in a number of various directions and thus direct and steer our life-boat.

In our daily lives we can turn in many different directions. When we begin to view life as a spiritual journey we find that, although outwardly we can move in many directions, inwardly our movement is in either of two directions. Jesus said: "Love one another as I have loved you." Upon hearing these words, we now have a decision to make: whether to love or not to love.

A similar example can be found in an act of faith or belief. Peter, Jesus' disciple, is able to walk on water when he has faith and then he sinks when he stops believing (Matthew 15:26–32). Peter's decision was rather clear-cut: doubt or believe.

The Buddha also gives a clear example of the two options available to the spiritually aware:

Follow not after vanity, nor after the enjoyment of love and lust. He who is earnest and meditative obtains ample joy.

—II:27

The Buddha's statement presents two clear choices: the way of the "ego," of "me and mine," or an expansive awareness achieved through meditation.

The first option, that of immediate gratification, revolves around each person seeking his or her own individual happiness through the pleasures of the senses. This focus necessitates one feeling a strong sense of separativity and individual bodily awareness. If I am to enjoy a sensual experience as much as possible, I must be as aware as possible of my own body and senses. This awareness clearly separates me from others. As this attitude continues, I begin to consider my pleasure as more important than that of others and, taken a step further, I begin to seek my pleasure even at the expense of others.

As we become more and more dependent upon our senses and possessions for satisfaction, we are no longer the controller of our senses and possessions but, rather, we become controlled by them. We begin to think that our existence and happiness depend on possessions and sensual pleasures. We then begin to worry and become anxious that our wants will not be fulfilled. Our sense of self and happiness becomes dependent upon our five senses and possessions. Jesus presented an option to this constant worry concerning ourselves. This option is an awareness of God.

So do not be anxious about what you will eat or what you will drink, and let not your mind be disturbed by these things.

For worldly people seek after all these things; and your Father knows that these things are also necessary for you.

*But seek the kingdom of God, and all these
things shall be added to you.*
*Do not be afraid, O little flock; for your
Father is pleased to give you the kingdom.*
LUKE 12:29–32

Jesus described a level of awareness in which
we can become conscious of the "Kingdom" of
the Father. This realm of perfection, this heaven,
includes the promise of immortality—an awareness of our eternal aspects, our soul.

The Chandogya Upanishad teaches that the
seeker should meditate upon and realize the following truths:

Thou art imperishable.
Thou art the changeless reality.
Thou art the source of life.

At each moment we need to choose whether
we want to move towards oneness or
separativity. Unlike the movement towards division and separation, the movement towards
the eternal begins with a feeling of unity and
oneness within our hearts.

Unlike the mind which functions through division and separation, the spiritual heart attains
a feeling of unity and identification. We begin
to feel the living presence of God, not only within
ourselves, but within all of creation.

By feeling the soul-essence in each aspect of creation we become aware of the connection we all share regardless of outer differences defined by race, creed or sex. By looking beyond the temporal, transitory level of existence, we can begin to find the timeless unity in all of creation. Jesus spoke of this awareness as a form of rebirth:

Truly, truly, I say to you, if a man is not born of water and the spirit, he cannot enter into the kingdom of God.

What is born of flesh is flesh; and what is born of the spirit is spirit.

Do not be surprised because I have told you that you all must be born again.

—JOHN 3:5–8

This re-birth into an awareness of the essence-spirit and unity in all of creation is not an act of thought or the adoption of a certain belief system, but rather the emergence of an actual awareness, a direct experience. There is a great difference between believing there is a city called Rome and the actual experience of being in Rome, experiencing the actual city. Jesus affirms this when he says:

Truly, truly, I say to you, we speak only what we know, and we testify only to what we have seen. . .

—JOHN 3:11

The experience of unity that can be felt within the spiritual heart is described in mystical literature from many cultures and times. It is an actual experience and not the result of mental constructions. People who delude themselves with mental fabrications of spiritual attainments, sooner or later, suffer some degree of psychological breakdown.

If we choose to move towards the feeling described by Sri Chinmoy as "the union-aspiring heart," the first step is becoming aware of our own spiritual depths and then becoming aware of that depth in others. This is attained through prayer, meditation and self-reflection. Jesus taught:

> *. . . clean first the inside of the cup and of the plate, so that their outside may also be clean.*
> —MATTHEW 23:26

Our awareness must transcend the physical realm. The Katha Upanishad recommends:

> *His form is not to be seen, no one beholds him with the eye. He is imagined by the heart by wisdom, by the mind. Those who know this are immortal.*

Each action of ours, each thought and feeling can be seen as a movement either towards division or oneness. In order to help mankind, spiritual teachers have, throughout history, pointed us in the direction of oneness. The great teachers never force their will or opinion on others, rather they speak to those wishing to learn. Jesus offered advice which individuals and nations would be wise to follow:

> *. . . return the sword to its place; for all who take swords will die by swords.*
>
> —MATTHEW 26:52

Spiritual teachers offer the beauty and immensity of their realization to all who are interested. If we decide to direct our lives towards oneness with all of creation, they will be there to guide and help us with our decisions.

> *Come to me, all you who labor and carry burdens, and I will give you rest.*
>
> *Take my yoke upon you, and learn from me, for I am gentle and meek in my heart, and you will find rest for your souls.*
>
> —MATTHEW 11:28–29

The Buddha, 500 years earlier, offered seekers the same message:

> *He who takes refuge with Buddha, the Law and the Order; he who with clear understand-*

ing seeks the four noble truths. . . is delivered
from all suffering.

—XIV:190–192

Lao Tzu, knowing nature to be a dance of one-ness and synchronicity offered this simple bit of advice: "Leave all things to follow their natural course, and do not interfere." It is always the division-mind that interferes with life's oneness-heart.

At every moment
We have to decide
Whether we want
The division-desiring mind
Or the union-aspiring heart.

Suggested Readings

Aurobindo, Sri. *The Message of the Gita* (India: Sri Aurobindo Ashman Press, 1938).

Brown, Brian. *The Wisdom of the Chinese* (Garden City Publishing Co. Inc., New York, 1920).

Chinmoy, Sri.
(Please note: Sri Chinmoy has authored over 1000 books encompassing a wide range of expression from spiritual stories, plays, philosophy, poetry, commentaries, lectures, mythology to songs. Just ask for his works at your local bookstore or contact: New York: Aum Publications.)

The Dhammapada. Translated by Irving Babbit (New York: New Directions Publishing Corporation, 1936).

Holy Bible: From the Ancient Eastern Text. Translated by George M. Lamsa. (San Francisco: Harper, 1933).

Lao Tzu *Tao Te Ching: The Way of Life.* Translated by Raymond B. Blackney (New York: New American Library, 1955).

Lao Tzu *Tao Teh Ching.* Translated by Dr. John C. H. Wu (New York: St. John's University Press, 1973).

Prabhavananda, Swami. *The Song of God: Bhagavad-Gita* (New York: Signet, 1944).

Prabhavananda, Swami. *The Upanishads: Breath of the Eternal* (Hollywood; Vedanta Press, 1947).

Radhakrishnan, S. *The Bhagavadgita* (San Francisco: Harper & Row, 1948).

The Upanishads. Translated by Max Müller (New York: Dover Publications, 1962 [first published in 1879]).